# PRAISE FOR
# THE CONFIDENCE CODE FOR GIRLS

"Girl power depends on self-confidence, but many girls struggle to see how awesome they really are. The good news is there are steps girls can take to build their confidence—not by twisting themselves into knots, but by gaining new mental tools and embracing their authentic selves. I wish I had this book when I was a girl—and I'm really glad today's girls have it now."

—SHERYL SANDBERG, COO of Facebook and
founder of Lean In and Option B

"This is the book every girl needs to make her dreams come true."

—LAURIE HERNANDEZ, US Olympic gold medalist and
bestselling author of *I Got This: To Gold and Beyond*

"An essential read for every girl in her tween years. This book encourages girls to take action despite unhelpful thinking patterns, to be unafraid of failure, and to challenge the worries that hold so many girls back. Presented in a relatable and engaging manner, it also provides excellent guidance on navigating the often judgmental and provoking world of social media. Girls will develop a much deeper understanding of what it means to be themselves and express that confidently. I am inspired by what the authors have done in offering such a tremendous guidebook that girls will reference time and time again in their journey to forming a solid, confident self."

—DR. BONNIE ZUCKER, licensed psychologist and author
of *Anxiety-Free Kids: An Interactive Guide for Parents and
Children*

"If you've ever wished you had the courage to say what you really think, or do the thing that scares you, this is the book for you! Confidence is crucial for girls today, and Katty and Claire have figured out the recipe. Their advice is realistic and practical. Reading this book will help you change your life—and the world!"

—RACHEL SIMMONS, *New York Times* bestselling author of *Enough As She Is*, *Odd Girl Out*, and *The Curse of the Good Girl* and leadership expert at Smith College

"Girls should know it's cool to be different. I learned that lesson on the ice, playing hockey. I didn't always fit in, but I came to embrace that, and it gave me confidence. This book can help every girl flip that switch in her head, so she can feel the awesomeness and confidence that come from being unique."

—HILARY KNIGHT, Olympic silver medalist and member of the US women's national ice hockey team

"Wow!!! I love love love this book for girls. Every single day I work with girls who suffer so much because they don't have the tools *The Confidence Code for Girls* provides. It gives tweens tips and tools to manage everything from stress to self-doubt to sticky social situations. Adults will appreciate the book's focus on empowerment and concrete action steps, and girls will love the humor, stories, and fun activities. Whether you're a parent or an educator, this is an invaluable resource."

—PHYLLIS L. FAGELL, school counselor, author, and contributor to the *Washington Post*'s On Parenting column

# THE CONFIDENCE CODE FOR GIRLS

## TAKING RISKS, **MESSING UP**, & BECOMING YOUR AMAZINGLY imperfect, TOTALLY POWERFUL SELF

### KATTY KAY & CLAIRE SHIPMAN

**WITH JILLELLYN RILEY**

**ILLUSTRATED BY NAN LAWSON**

**HARPER**
*An Imprint of HarperCollins Publishers*

Library of Congress Control Number: 2017949549
ISBN 978-0-06-279698-1

Typography by ebb-n-flo and Alison Klapthor
18 19 20 21 22  PC/LSCH  10 9 8 7 6 5 4 3 2 1
❖
First Edition

For my mum,
the fabulously impressive,
amazingly inspiring,
totally awesome
Shirley Kay

—K.K.


For my female confidence gurus:
my mother, Christie Shipman,
who broke rules with regular, joyful abandon;
my mother-in-law, Linda Dryden,
who was always game for any leap;
and my daughter, Della Carney,
whose bravery and clarity
I work to emulate every single day

—C.S.

# CONTENTS

# MEET OUR CONFIDENCE GUIDES

# AUTHORS' NOTE

KATTY     CLAIRE

Y ou know that feeling you get when you do something brave? That incredible energy when you find your courage and try something that's not easy? That's . . .

## CONFIDENCE.

Confidence gives you the power, the lift, the oomph to be yourself and do what you want—even when it's scary.

What's it like to *have* confidence? We talked to dozens of girls of all ages for this book, and here's how confidence makes them feel:

A few years ago, we wrote a book about women and confidence. When it became a bestseller, we realized that tons of women wanted to know more about this incredible energy source, to live bolder, braver, more confident lives. We learned so many fascinating things doing the research—we found out that even rats have confidence, for example, and that scientists can measure it! But the most important thing we did was crack the code for confidence—in other words, we learned how to make it.

Now we're excited to pass the Confidence Code on to you. Researchers have found that the tween and teen years are the best time for confidence creation. We've packed this book with stories, quizzes, illustrations, and other fun stuff. And you should also know that everything here is based on what the smartest scientists and experts in the world know about confidence and where it comes from.

Remember Imani, Kayla, and Alex—the three characters you met earlier in the hallway of their school? They could all use a confidence boost. You might have noticed that they sound worried, afraid to try new things, and unable to be fully themselves. You'll see the three of them in action throughout the book. We want them, and you, to say "Why not?" instead of "No way!" whenever you see a challenge.

We should warn you—confidence gets addictive. Once you have a taste, you'll want more. And more. So let's get going. Before you know it, you'll have learned to build your own Confidence Code, and you'll be doing things you never even imagined.

# WHAT YOU CAN EXPECT ALONG THE WAY . . .

**Girls of Action:**

Real girls who've unleashed their confidence and done some amazing things

**Confidence Close-ups:**

Real stories from girls in the midst of the ugly, scary process of confidence creation. We changed their names.

**Confidence Warm-ups:**

Activities we want you to try when you put the book down to pump up your confidence

## Confidence Quizzes:

Based on real stuff girls and experts told us about, these teasers train your brain to be more confident.

## Confidence Conundrums:

Broad, puzzling questions for you to tackle that don't always have obvious answers

## Quick Quotes:

Real quotes from real girls, meant to make you think or wonder or smile

## Your Turn:

Things we want you to notice

SECTION 1

# THE
# KEYS
# TO
# CONFIDENCE

# KAYLA'S BIG RISK, PART 1

## TO BE CONTINUED . . .

# CHAPTER 1

## THE NUTS & BOLTS OF CONFIDENCE

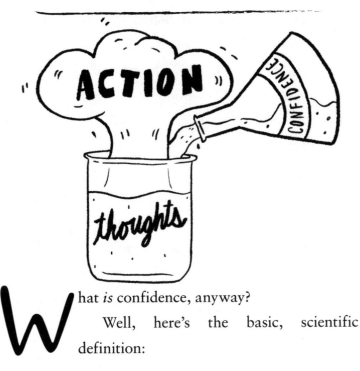

What *is* confidence, anyway?

Well, here's the basic, scientific definition:

**Confidence is what turns our *thoughts* into *action*.**

**You can also think of it like a math formula:**
**Thoughts + Confidence = Action.**

**Or picture a chemistry set, with thoughts in one beaker and confidence in another. Combine them and, POOF! You get exciting, explosive action.**

Confidence is what you use to help you do anything that seems **hard, scary, or impossible**. We're not necessarily talking about extreme actions like jumping off a cliff. (Or maybe we are, as long as you have a hang glider or parachute!) Confidence is what gives you a boost for everyday challenges as well. It's what Kayla used to get herself to those basketball tryouts in the first part of "Kayla's Big Risk."

Imagine confidence as a tiny, powerful coach inside your mind helping you do all the things you want to do. *"I know you're thinking you can't put your hand up in class today, but come on, I've seen you do it a million times before. Ignore those nerves and just throw your hand up there. You can do it."*

 **QUIZ**

**Which of these actions requires confidence?**

1. Eve has a best friend, Hannah, and they're practically twins. When they're hanging out together, they always just get each other. But then one day Hannah says something a little mean about Eve's new haircut. Eve

feels betrayed, but she doesn't want to tell Hannah she's upset because she's afraid of feeling awkward about it. Still, she goes ahead and brings it up with her and is honest about how she's been feeling.

2. Cate's a fantastic math student. She's always loved numbers—they just make sense to her. She works hard at math and flies through the homework. Her teacher tells her that she would absolutely make the mathletes team if she wanted to. She tries out, and it's a dream come true—wall-to-wall math problems!

3. Isabella knows every part of *Beauty and the Beast*, the upcoming school musical, by heart. She loves to sing, but she's never been in a show before and lots of the other kids have. She's also not sure about her voice because she's never really practiced. And the auditions are in front of all those other kids who want a part, too. Still, she pushes herself to try out! . . . But the audition is just as hideously embarrassing as she expected.

# Answers: Let's Break It Down

If you answered #1, #3, or both, you're TOTALLY right. The girl who talked to her friend and the girl who tried out for the play did something that clearly required confidence. Number 2 required a bit of confidence, too, but not as much.

1. Eve did a hard thing in talking to Hannah, who was upset for about an hour after Eve confessed her feelings. They both learned to be more honest with each other and sensitive about what they say in the future.

2. Cate tried out and made the mathletes, but she didn't do something that hard, did she? She basically kept doing something she's *already good at doing.* Let's see her take on a more challenging activity. *That* would require more confidence.

3. Isabella really stretched herself when she tried out. She didn't make it, and was bummed, but she realized afterward that she still wanted to be in a musical. She plans to prepare for the next audition differently. For one thing, she's going to start training her voice so that, when

she's nervous, it doesn't get thin and wavering. Lots of people didn't make it, and their lives aren't over. The important thing? She took a risk and took action.

The essential idea in all of these stories is ACTION. Think verbs and action words:

**Jumping off a high diving board**
**Talking to a neighbor about babysitting**
**Trying a new sport, like Kayla did**

Try something, do something, make something, join something, say something, be something. Get the picture?

Confidence is _____. (Fill in your action word here—unless this is a library book, or e-book, in which case make a list on paper or in your phone!)

**Girls of Action** have the most exciting lives ever. Why? Think about it: You can sit there and worry and watch things happening out in the world. *Or* you can jump in and be part of the fun, creating adventures and success by exploring and doing.

You want to try out for a team, even if you're not

so sure how good you are? Confidence will give you a boost. You want to write a blog and tell the whole world what you think, even though you worry you don't have interesting thoughts? Confidence is key for that, too. You want to be yourself, even if that self is totally different from all the other kids? Confidence makes it happen. You want to dye your hair or shave your head, skip dresses and wear what you want? Confidence . . . well, you know the rest. Ava, in the story below, uses her confidence to do something that's really important to her.

## CONFIDENCE CLOSE-UP

Ava loves to take pictures, using all kinds of apps and filters on her phone. She does it endlessly, posting photos on her Pinterest boards and on Instagram. For her birthday, she got a beautiful old camera. Now she is totally obsessed. She practices on everything around her all the time: cracks in the sidewalk, the sky, litter blowing down the street, gates, bicycles. But what she really wants to do is take pictures of people. She is fascinated by people—all the different shapes and sizes of them, from chubby babies to wrinkly old ladies. It's rude to take people's pictures without permission, she knows—and she's way too shy to approach strangers and ask them. But she's longing to snap that fascinating guy with the tiny mustache waiting for a bus, or the woman juggling armloads of groceries while strutting down the street. Ava practices what she could say to them. A couple of times, she does manage to walk up to a stranger, but immediately panics and turns away. That makes it worse because she's mad at herself for not even trying.

In the park one day, Ava is watching some women doing tai chi, their arms raised gracefully toward the sky. She can't stand it any longer—she's tired of missing out on what she wants to do! Ava shakes her head to clear the panic, takes a deep breath, and approaches the women, telling them she loves the way their shadows look with the sun behind them. She asks if she can take their pictures, and they say yes! Ava ends up shooting some of her favorite images ever. It's still not easy for her to go up to people on the street, and when she does, plenty of people are rude and crabby. But as people start to agree, her pile of photos grows, and so does her confidence.

## USING CONFIDENCE

Of course, different people will need confidence for different things. The many girls we spoke with gave us a big and varied list.

> *"Asking my friend why she cropped me out of a picture on Instagram."*

> *"Telling people I'm gay and not hiding any part of myself."*

> *"Speaking up about bullying, even if kids get mad at me."*

> *"Trying out for track, even if I only run when I'm late."*

"Staying quiet, knowing how to listen, and not making it all about me."

"Speaking up in class."

"Showing people the real me. They might not like me."

"Going to gym class. I am afraid of looking totally uncoordinated."

"Telling my friends I want to be by myself. But I don't have the nerve to say no when they want to hang out."

"Meeting new people. It's scary."

## CONFIDENCE WARM-UP

Now YOU take a crack at it. First of all, gather the tools you'll need to start building your own Confidence Code: a pen or pencil, and a notebook or journal (a stack of loose paper works, too). You can also use your phone, if you have one, to keep track of stuff if you'd rather, though scientists have found that writing things down imprints them on our brains better. Whatever you choose, this is your Confidence Notebook. You might be rolling your eyes and groaning about extra homework, but this isn't math or history, after all; it's about you being AWESOME.

Start by thinking of the things that really challenge you, the things that might take more confidence, and jot them down. On another page, write down the things you are good at doing. Here's an example:

| Like to Do | Hard for Me |
| --- | --- |
| Lacrosse | Science test |
| Video games | Talking to a waiter |
| Science labs | Just being me |

Sometimes it does take huge amounts of confidence *just to be yourself.* At your age, feelings are bigger, stakes seem higher, and your impulses can be confusing. You have the urge to define yourself and show independence, but it also feels absolutely essential to FIT IN. And what about when you're facing other realities that might make you feel different? If you're one of only a few girls of color at your school, for example, it can take confidence and courage to show up as yourself instead of trying to fit into a mold. And for LGBTQ kids, deciding to talk about what you're feeling and who you really are for sure requires confidence, since it may not be what other people are used to. Anytime you challenge what seems "normal" to most people, you need confidence in who you are at your core.

## CONFIDENCE IMPOSTERS

You probably know this already, but sometimes the people who *seem* the most confident aren't confident at all.

## Power Positions

Want some quick confidence? Try this power position: Stand up and hold your arms outstretched, like you're trying to touch the walls on either side of you. Press your palms out, like you are a stop sign. Hold it. KEEP holding it for three minutes: count to sixty really slowly three times. (It's a workout, too!)

Or, just focus on sitting up straight! We know, that one sounds like something your grandmother might say, but scientists we interviewed found that both of those moves can increase your feeling of power and give you a temporary confidence boost!

19

## IMPOSTER BEHAVIOR

♦ Being phony, bratty, or arrogant

♦ Having the loudest voice in the room and talking over your friends

♦ Making other people feel bad and putting them down so that you can make yourself feel better

♦ Always getting your way

♦ Trying to look awesome so you can make everyone envious

♦ Being the BEST and making sure everyone knows you are the best

## ONE BIG THING THAT CONFIDENCE IS *NOT*: IT'S NOT ABOUT HOW YOU LOOK. IT'S ABOUT HOW YOU ACT, AND WHO YOU ARE.

## CONFIDENCE CLOSE-UP

Eleven-year-old Karah was proud of her long, wavy, thick hair. She tended to flip it around, making sure people noticed it, and she loved the attention. But when her cousin Ali got cancer and her hair fell out, Ali wanted a wig. Because of Ali's illness, Karah found out lots of people need wigs when they are being treated for cancer. She decided to cut her hair and donate it to make those wigs. She was scared that she would look weird, that people wouldn't think she was pretty anymore. But she really wanted to help someone who might need her pretty hair more than she did. So Karah cut off almost all of her hair. Not quite a buzz cut, but close to it. At first, she thought she looked ugly without her hair, and then after a few days, she felt powerful. She was more than her hair! She intends to grow it back, but who knows—once she does, maybe she'll cut it off and donate it again.

## CONFIDENCE WARM-UP

By now you're getting good at seeing what confidence is and what it's not. Start to spot it in the people around you.

1. **FIND ROLE MODELS**—other daring, incredible girls and women you know or have read about. What's

the best part of what they do? Write it down, because going back to it later will inspire you!

2. **LOOK OUT FOR FAKERS**—all those people who use counterfeit confidence to be mean or put other people down to puff themselves up. Fakers may roam the halls *acting like* they have confidence to spare, but that's phony, and you can spot it from a mile away.

3. **SHOUT IT OUT**—grab your phone and send a confidence compliment to three people you know. Like your friend who works at the recycling drive. Or your sister who stood up to a bully. Or your mom, who asked for a raise at work. Let them know that you *see* their confidence in action—that you *notice* what they do. Research shows that when you hand out that kind of a boost, you build your *own* confidence!

## MAKING MORE CONFIDENCE: THE BIG PICTURE

At this point, it should be pretty clear what confidence

is and why it matters so much. And you're probably thinking: *Duh, it's obviously great. But what if I don't exactly have buckets of confidence sitting around for that moment I want to try something? What if I want to try out for the debate team, and all I can think about is people staring at me, and I don't want to get off my couch?* Well, that's why knowing how to make it is so important.

Scientists have studied people's genetics and behavior for years. They now believe that while we're each born with some confidence, we can always make more. And here are the basic mechanics of doing that: when you take action, especially when you do something even slightly risky, you not only *use* confidence, but you also end up *creating more!*

Imagine some gears in your head. Confidence is the grease that helps you turn those gears of your thoughts and generate action. And the fabulous result? That action generates more confidence for next time.

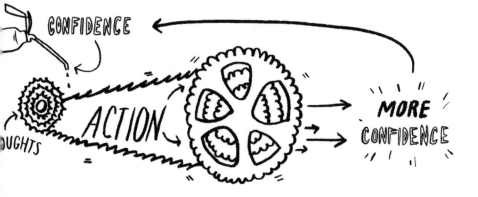

Action is fundamental to making your Confidence Code. In "Kayla's Big Risk," for example, Kayla doesn't yet realize that she's built more confidence simply by trying out for the basketball team, even though she didn't make it. She'll soon learn. But back to *you* sitting on that couch. Let's say you get up, try out for debate, and don't say the smartest things at the first session. You prepare a bit more for the next session. You get on the team as an alternate, take it seriously, and eventually make the team as a full member. *That* kind of process is what *really* builds up your confidence supply: all that trying, risking, messing up, struggling, and eventually getting good at something. Creating confidence is less about the result—the success or winning.

**It's more about the doing. You'd be much more likely to try out for other things now, since you have some confidence stored away. Try it and see.**

But we'd be kidding if we told you that the *doing* is super easy. How do you deal with the butterflies, the wanting to throw up, the feeling that you'd rather stay in bed or hide in your closet or sit glued to that couch?

How do you take that critical first step toward being a Girl of Action, toward building a confidence stockpile when you don't already have extra confidence to get the process going? Well, you have to RISK IT.

# GIRLS OF ACTION

Nine-year-old Gracie Kuglin has always loved all creatures, even the noncuddly ones like spiders and scorpions. She plans to be a vet when she grows up. She sold some of her old toys and used the money to buy toys for the dogs at the Humane Society. Then she found out that the Humane Society branch in her North Dakota hometown was desperately short on money for essentials like vaccines and food. That's when Gracie knew she wanted to figure out a way to raise more money to benefit these animals. Even five dollars can make a difference—it can feed fifteen animals for a day or pay for a vaccination.

Her grandma was having a garage sale, so Gracie and her mom decided that would be the perfect opportunity for a lemonade stand. Gracie can be shy about talking to people, but she was determined to help these animals. Once she gets it in her head to do something, she definitely does it! People came from more than twenty miles away to donate to Gracie's stand, including the principal of her school and several teachers.

For her next step, Gracie has even bigger plans. "They need a new dog fence," she told us. "They need dog toys, dog and cat food—they need a lot of stuff!" So for her birthday, she's asking her friends to bring gifts for the Humane Society rather than for her. And she's expanding her next lemonade stand to include a bake sale. She says she's surprised herself by how bold she could be on behalf of her furry friends who couldn't speak for themselves.

# CHAPTER 2

## RISKY BUSINESS!

Taking a risk is like taking a big leap of faith. It's using whatever confidence you have, and maybe some courage and bravery as well, to sail over the dark abyss of whatever scares you.

Just listen to how different dictionaries describe risk:

**risk:**

1. **the possibility something bad or unpleasant will happen**

2. **a chance of getting hurt or losing something**

3. **peril**

*Peril? Getting hurt?* Um, no wonder our instinct is to avoid risk. But remember: action, especially action that's hard, is what builds confidence. Risk is exactly what Kayla confronts in "Kayla's Big Risk" (yes, the title kind of gives it away). She worries about embarrassing herself, or failing. But she goes for it after getting help and good advice from her friends—*"What do you have to lose?"*

Sometimes, if you don't have a supply of confidence, you have to rely on boosts like that, or even sheer will, to fuel your first move. But once you start, you'll get into a confidence-creating zone pretty quickly. In this chapter we'll offer you a **seven-step plan** to get you through your early risk-taking jitters. One girl we talked with, Lucy, said she "totally hates risky stuff" and "wanted to puke," but she finally figured out how to take a leap.

## CONFIDENCE CLOSE-UP

Starting when she was eleven, Lucy had a regular babysitting gig, taking care of a little boy while his parents did laundry or caught up on chores around

## Your Risk List

Make a list of five risks you want to take. Nothing huge. No saving the world, quitting school, or telling that annoying history teacher what he can do with his textbook. Scientists have found that when people take the time to write down a goal, they are 42 percent more likely to make it a reality. So, what are things that you've had on your mind, but that seem a little hard or risky? Try a new instrument? Talk to that funny kid in your class? Get your Confidence Notebook, or a scrap of paper, and take the risk of just declaring them. That *already* means they're more possible.

the house. But after a couple of years, the boy's parents started having her babysit at night when they went out. Lucy got to do the whole bath time/story time/bedtime thing. It was fun but also lots more work and responsibility.

Lucy realized she wanted to ask the parents to pay her more. But the thought of actually having that conversation made her anxious. She really liked them, and they were always nice to her and left great snacks. . . . What if they got mad? What if they got offended, thinking that she didn't like the little kid? What if they thought she didn't deserve more? Her stomach hurt just thinking about the conversation.

By talking the situation through with her own parents, she figured out a way to bring it up. She also made a mental list of what she could say: "I love working here. And I feel confident that I'm doing a good job. My responsibilities have gotten bigger, and I think it would be fair for me to start charging more money."

So ... when the boy's parents returned after a movie one night, Lucy blurted it all out. Maybe not as perfectly as she'd practiced it in her head, but she put it out there. Immediately she felt better. And the parents totally agreed, coughing up more money on the spot. They even said they felt bad about not thinking of it themselves. They still called her to babysit just as often, and the whole process allowed her to create some confidence.

Lucy took a risk, and it paid off. And maybe this story makes it sound pretty straightforward—but we know it's not always that easy. These steps will help you build your appetite for risk-taking:

## STEP 1: EMBRACING RISK

Before you can go out and attempt a lot of risk-taking yourself, you really have to believe in the benefits. Almost every situation you face will hand you choices. And often the most frightening choice is the right one.

 **QUIZ**

**How good are you at spotting the *upsides* of a risky move?**

1. *Jaylen is new to her Arizona middle school and hasn't made any friends yet. She's noticed a group of girls in the cafeteria who seem fun, and she thinks one of them smiled at her the other day—maybe even waved her over. Should Jaylen:*

   a. Try wandering over one day at lunch, even if they shut her out?

   b. Think about it for another week or so, see whether they show any more signs of friendliness, and then try?

   c. Resign herself to being alone for a few

months? No chance of utter embarrassment that way.

2. *Libby loves animals. She spent a fantastic week on a school project at an animal shelter, and she came up with an idea for matching abandoned dogs and cats with nursing homes, like the one where her grandmother lives. The residents get so happy when animals visit.* Should she:

   a. Do more research, and maybe propose it when she's older and has more information? She could probably learn a lot that way.

   b. Just focus on her homework and leave this to the grown-ups? She'd avoid risk of humiliation.

   c. Head over and speak with the director, even though talking to an adult she doesn't know makes her nervous and there are probably a million reasons why it won't work?

# Answers: Let's Break It Down

1. **A** is the real risk Jaylen should take. Her gut says the girls will be friendly. And she'll never

know if she waits too long. **B** might work, but she also might miss her chance. **C** is clearly not a good move!

2.  **C** is where Libby would take the biggest risk, and it's the best move. **A** could work, but it's so cautious. She doesn't really need to perfect her idea. She might learn a lot from the director if she tries now. As for **B**—don't get us started.

## STEP 2: DECIDE WHETHER IT'S A SMART OR DUMB RISK

This part isn't that hard. We want you to embrace *smart* risks. We're not talking about diving into the shallow end of a pool or giving out your address to someone online you don't know. Don't do anything that feels wrong or that someone else is pressuring you to do.

Smart risks are things that you might typically shy away from but that, in your gut, you know could increase the fun, adventure, and powerful parts of your life. Think about both Jaylen and Libby. They might be disappointed or temporarily embarrassed if they take these risks. But smart risks usually pay off eventually, even if they don't work right away (more on dealing with that in the failure chapter).

 **QUIZ**

**These risks are straight from the mouths of girls we talked to. What do you think—are they smart or dumb?**

1. "Joining a new club. It seems scary, but fun."
2. "Sneaking my phone out during school."
3. "Posting a picture of me and my friend on Instagram, even though I didn't ask her first."
4. "Talking to new people."
5. "Trying out a new move on my soccer team but falling on my butt."
6. "Running for student council to protest the dress code."
7. "Letting my teacher know she graded my test wrong."
8. "Letting my BFF know she hurt my feelings."

9. "Reading my poem out loud to our class."
10. "Skipping school with my friends to hang out at the mall."

# Answers: Let's Break It Down

To us, most of these seem like terrific, smart risks. EXCEPT for numbers 2, 3, and 10.

#2: Breaking a school rule is likely to get you in trouble. Just wait to use your phone until later.

#3: Posting a pic on Instagram without permission might *seem* OK, but the right thing to do is ask your friend. So much easier to avoid a problem before it happens.

#10: Well, it pretty much goes without saying: skipping school is not a brilliant move.

## STEP 3: COMFORT ZONE = DANGER ZONE

Of course, the very hardest part of risk is leaving your comfort zone. After all, our comfort zone is just so, well, cozy and comfy. Picture it now, your very own CZ. It's warm and inviting, full of beanbag chairs and gigantic plushy pillows. Or maybe twinkling lights and plenty of snacks and your furry dog or cat.

We all have them—safe little pockets. It's so much easier to stick with what you know. Not rock any boats. So much nicer to hang out with the friends you already have, who are already chill. Why not just hide there? The girls in our next Confidence Close-up told us that for a long time, they *never* wanted to venture out of their CZs.

## CONFIDENCE CLOSE-UP

Wyatt loves to draw. She's never happier than when she's hunched over in the art room, scribbling away amid clouds of charcoal dust. She doodles in the margins of every sheet of paper that comes her way and covers all the junk mail in her house with her sketches. Sometimes she thinks sketching with a group, maybe making comics together, might be cool. But Wyatt is so comfy within the colors and swirls of her own art zone that she stays put.

Feng is an outfielder on her softball team. She has the whole right field to herself and she's super comfy out there. The girls who play first base and shortstop are awesome, so balls rarely come to her. When they do, there's plenty of time to get under them. She plays her position well, and never has to deal with feeling nervous. She isn't eager to shake things up and try a different position.

OK, we all need our comfort zones. But we have to be able to leave them to take on new challenges. If we stay, it could get suffocating or boring. Even though doing anything for the first time is scary, trying new things is how you keep learning about yourself and finding out what else you might like. If you'd stayed in your baby comfort zone, you'd still be sitting on a blanket, waiting for all the food and toys to come to you. INSTEAD, you pulled yourself up and started toddling around to see what the world has to offer. Keep exploring!

## STEP 4: WHAT'S RISKY TO YOU?

Risks are different for everyone. Start to narrow your mental risk list. Zoom in on what makes *you* nervous.

### QUIZ

**What seems risky?**
    a. Camping
    b. Performing in a band
    c. Having a lab partner you don't know

Or what is scary?

   a. Water slides and roller coasters

   b. Trying out for a team

   c. Sharing a song you wrote with other people

**Any of these make you feel sick to your stomach?**

   a. Skiing

   b. Giving a presentation to your class

   c. Submitting your drawing for the yearbook
cover

# Answers: Let's Break It Down

If you picked mostly **A**s, then physical actions likely tend to make you nervous. If you picked mostly **B**s, then performance seems risky to you. And if you chose **C**s, then it looks like sharing something with the world, being vulnerable with strangers, feels like the bigger risk to you.

And keep this in mind—risk varies for different kinds of kids. Immigrants from other countries, for example, can face challenges that can make their daily lives feel full of risk. Maybe it's about a struggle to speak English, or maybe it's about looking different from the people around them. Farrah is from Yemen and wears a hijab, a traditional Muslim head scarf, in her suburban school. Nobody else has one, so for her, simply going to school can feel scary or risky, knowing some people are staring at her. She reminds herself she has a right to be there, like everyone else. And maybe the staring is not mean, just curious. That makes her feel better, and she tries to show them that she is really just like they are.

For kids who are in wheelchairs, or are blind, or deal with anything that makes navigating the world a little trickier, taking a risk is a whole other ball game. It's a constant battle to navigate the physical world and a constant battle to ignore other people's staring.

## STEP 5: SMALL STEPS

Researchers have figured out that when you think about a BIG challenge, it can seem overwhelming. *"How the heck do I get from where I am to all the way over there? Ugh, I might as well quit now."* They've also discovered that when you pause for a few minutes and break the challenge down into a bunch of small steps, it's lots more achievable.

For example, when Lucy wanted to talk to those parents about her babysitting, she broke it down. Her goal was to be paid more money. Asking for it seemed almost impossible—until she divided it into four steps. She listed her reasons, and then she talked to her parents and rehearsed her lines with them. Finally, she picked a time to bring it up. She didn't do it all perfectly, but having a plan and small things to do along the way helped. Sometimes it helps to start with some **bridge challenges**—a series of little risks, like little bridges, that will eventually lead you out of your CZ and right over all of the scary stuff you've been imagining.

## CONFIDENCE CLOSE-UP

Wyatt, the girl who was living in her art comfort zone, started small. She was tired of being by herself all the time, but she only wanted to open herself up to other people bit by bit. First, she spent a few weeks thinking. She imagined a gathering of people who liked the same kind of stuff she liked, who wanted to draw or make comics, sketching and coming up with funny captions. Ultimately she felt a little bolder and came up with the idea of an art magazine. The next move was the big one. She put up a poster at her school announcing the new magazine and invited other kids to join in. At first, nobody signed up and she felt miserable walking by that pathetic poster with its empty sign-up spaces. But then one kid, and then one more, and then another THREE kids put their names down and came to meet Wyatt at lunch. Now they're working on their first edition, full of totally out-there drawings and cartoons. It'll be scary to make a bunch of copies and hand them out to strangers, but it's better than sitting all alone in the back of the room.

## STEP 6: GET COMFORTABLE BEING UNCOMFORTABLE

Risk isn't usually fun. It can be very, very uncomfortable. But you will get used to it. It's like eating something you've never tried, wearing something new, or getting over a fear of dogs. The only thing that works is eating a little bit over and over, or wearing that shirt a few times until it feels familiar, or learning to approach and pet dogs again and again. Sticking with stuff that doesn't always feel good is literally like vaccinating yourself— it's a big shot in the arm against future nerves. Naomi told us how she learned to tolerate severe discomfort and how she made her pain and fear work for her eventually.

## CONFIDENCE CLOSE-UP

Naomi spends hours riding horses. It can be risky and dangerous sitting atop an animal so huge and heavy, but she loves it and wants to be really good. She went to an intense camp where she was given a horse named Lulu. Lulu was totally wild and nearly ruined riding for her. For five days in a row, the horse kept bucking and knocking Naomi off. Or the horse would pull down to nibble the grass, making it hard for Naomi to lead her. And she was in SO much pain from all the falls—her back felt broken and she had purple and green bruises all over. It might seem like what Naomi was stockpiling was a bunch of hurt and humiliation, but all that week she was building confidence because she was sticking with it.

One time, Naomi fell so hard the wind was knocked out of her. She was curled in a ball on the ground thinking, "I give up. Forget it. I hate this. I am going to ask for an easier horse." But once she got up again and nothing was broken, she realized she had to stick with it—if she gave up now, all that pain, all those falls, would be for NOTHING. She realized she was feeling stronger, if nothing else. And, she told herself, the worst had likely already happened! So she kept going, imagining herself as a graceful, strong rider on a beautiful, powerful animal, in sync and connected. Pretty soon, she started riding without fear. If she could handle getting thrown by Lulu, she could handle anything!

## STEP 7: BE YOUR OWN COACH

When you're finally ready for action, you've got to learn to be your own coach. Here are some tricks of the trade.

◆ *Visualize*. Picture in your mind what you want to happen, what it will really look like. Time to move beyond the *what ifs* and focus on *what it will be*. All the big athletes and singers use visualization to get from practices and rehearsals to big moments on the court or on stage. It's what Naomi did on her horse. Scientists have found that by visualizing what you WANT to happen, you're more likely to MAKE it happen. Really!

◆ *Talk yourself up*. Here are some micro–confidence boosts to help you leap. Keep these phrases handy, and use them often.

"I've done stuff like this before, and I can do it again."

"What's the worst that can happen?"

"I've got this."

"I can handle it."

"No problem."

◊ *Practice*. Repetition makes it all feel natural, like it's just part of what you do, not a huge stretch. Rehearse what you want to say or what you want to do. No need to overdo it. But some prep is really useful.

◊ *Pick your team*. Every coach knows a great team is essential. You need to know who's in your corner—which adults and friends will give you the kind of support Kayla got. Start a list and double-check it when you read the friendship chapter.

◊ *Remember this story*. One scientist who studies confidence told us that he noticed men kept scoring much better on a puzzle-solving math test he had given many times. Then he studied the women's answers closely. He noticed something. They were skipping a lot of the questions! He realized that when the women were unsure, they often wouldn't take a risk and guess. He told the next group of men and women that EVERYONE had to answer ALL the questions. What happened? The scores were almost identical. So, not taking a risk, not acting, has consequences.

◊ *Game time.* Time for action. If none of the above has worked, and you're still terrified, tell yourself you're going to DO IT AFRAID. It's a powerful phrase we got from a young girl in New Mexico. Because you can't always wait for those nerves to vanish. What if they don't? So *admit* you're nervous, but *decide* to act anyway. Shrug and declare: "I'm going to just do it afraid." You have the power to do it.

## CONFIDENCE CLOSE-UP

Feng eventually decided to start pushing herself, because standing in that softball outfield got really dull. Counting the clouds and watching other girls make exciting plays stopped being fun. She knew that she hated the pressure of diving for a ball (and usually missing it!), so she thought, "What if I were way better at doing that?" She started practicing. She spent hours throwing a ball against the side of her house and then racing to catch it. She was definitely getting more comfortable, but the idea of doing it FOR REAL in a game made her feel queasy. Still, when the girl at first base got injured midgame and they needed a sub, the coach waved Feng over and she decided to just run into position despite her nerves, without giving herself a chance to reconsider. Time for action, even if she still thought she might puke. She did miss a ball. Actually, she missed a bunch of balls. But she caught a bunch of other ones and had a blast. And now she's excited for next season. Who knows—maybe she'll try pitching!

Feng took a risk, fumbled a bit, but did fine. And now, in her mind, some exciting doors have opened.

What she really discovered is what we hope you see, too—there's no way to *think* yourself into being confident while *sitting* in your comfort zone. Action and risk are required, and usually—we hate to say this, so we'll make the print really small—some failure too.

## GIRLS OF ACTION

Amaiya Zafar is used to risk and struggle. She's always been pretty small, and when she told her friends, at thirteen, that she was taking up boxing, they rolled their eyes and said, "Yeah, right." As a nurse, her mom had doubts, too, worrying that it would be dangerous. But, Amaiya says, "Then my mom started to see how boxing helped me hold my head up high."

It also hasn't been easy for Amaiya to box in her hijab, the traditional Muslim head covering she's always worn. That's been more controversial than she imagined. She was disqualified from her amateur bout because she wouldn't take it off. "My hijab is my crown. When I walk down the street, I automatically get respect. I value it with my whole heart. I would feel like I'm missing something essential."

After a two-year struggle, USA Boxing finally gave her permission to wear it—but the International Boxing Association still hasn't. So she can't box in any Olympic qualifying matches.

Still, she keeps pounding away at her grueling workout schedule—ferociously competitive—often beating bigger opponents, even men. "I've always wanted to beat the boys at everything," she laughs. She hopes her battles in and out of the ring can be an inspiration to other girls.

"Boxing is my whole life," she says. "Everything I do revolves around boxing. And my hijab is my whole life. I don't want to have to compromise one for the other."

# CHAPTER 3

## EPIC FAIL

The *F*-word. It strikes fear in almost every heart, right? Nobody thinks they're supposed to say it. Or talk about it. Or even admit it can happen. You know the word we mean.

### FAILURE

There. It's on the page, on purpose. It's important to get used to the idea of failing. Not because it's fun; we're not going to pretend anyone ever loves failing—we certainly don't. But it's a natural result of risk-taking, it's part of building confidence, and it's going to happen to you, because it happens to EVERYONE.

## CONFIDENCE CLOSE-UP

Getting up on stage to act definitely made twelve-year-old Helen nervous. But once she got into it, she usually calmed down. And then afterward, she felt so great! But when she was assigned a monologue for the huge show at the end of summer camp, she started to panic. It was so boring and so long.

Helen studied and memorized and quizzed herself for days. Right up until the moment she walked in front of the lights, she was drilling herself. The kid in front of her did his thing, and then it was down to Helen. She stood up, opened her mouth—and nothing came out. Absolutely nothing. Her whole brain was a deep, dark hole without a glimmer of that monologue anywhere. This was not a case of one flubbed line or talking too fast or forgetting to breathe. This was a nightmare. The audience was full of parents, her mother was shooting a video, but absolutely nothing would come out of her mouth. All she could do was lamely point her finger at the next kid and then stumble off the stage. She felt like she couldn't face her parents, grandparents, or even her little brother ever again. She had totally, completely, publicly failed.

Most of us have had an epic fail like Helen's, and it's the worst. But Helen's incredibly painful, humiliating experience wasn't *all* bad.

*Wait, what?* you might ask. *What could possibly be* **good** *about it?*

Well, there's actual science showing that failure, of all things, helps to create success.

We know that may sound like a typically annoying adult thing to say. Because when your stomach is in knots and your mind is lurching, and you're free-falling into the fail zone, you're not thinking, "Great! More success for me!" You study, but still bomb the test; work hard on a paper, still get a bad grade; run for student council, but don't make it; strive to make that certain someone like you but—fail, fail, fail. There are so many ways to do it, and none of them feels good at the time.

But failure really does have an upside. It's not so much the failing, actually, but the recovery and learning that can be really valuable. It's all part of that critical confidence-building process we talked about earlier. The lessons of failure get stamped onto our brains, something scientists call *imprinting*, more deeply than other kinds of experiences. When you fail, you can learn a ton of useful stuff, if you pay attention.

# QUIZ

**How well do you understand the power of failure?**
*Annie barely makes it to school on time every day. It's hard for her to get up in the morning. She stays up late, her stuff is scattered everywhere, her clothes are all over her room. Her mother drags her out of bed each day*

and helps her find everything, and then she barrels into school seconds before the bell. It's soooooo stressful, and she hates getting there all sweaty and out of breath. Which of these will best change her habit?

a. Her mother stops waking her up. For three days in a row, she's actually late and she gets detention. Annie's furious at her mom.

b. Annie convinces her mom to get her a new alarm clock that records her own voice on it! Awesome; now she just has to remember to set it.

c. Annie makes a detailed plan on graph paper to get organized the night before, pack her stuff, and get herself up. She'll start next week.

## Answer: Let's Break It Down

For Annie, option **A**, as ugly as it sounds, turned out to be the one that worked. Here's what happened:

*After those three days of detention, Annie didn't want to be late ever again. Her room's organized, and her old alarm clock's set every night. (The cool new alarm clock had vanished under a pile of clothes by day three, and the fancy organizational chart never took off.) Failure made the difference.*

 **QUIZ**

**What's your failure style? Anything sound familiar?**

    a. You sob loudly into a furry pillow for hours and hours. And then you eat a carton of cookie-dough ice cream.

    b. Whatever. You're not even going to think about it. It. Never. Even. Happened.

    c. You feel sick. You want to puke, literally, wherever you are. And your head hurts. Ugh.

    d. You hole up in your room for a while, but you also know that after a few days you and everyone else will move on. It's awkward, but whatever.

    e. You want to hide, maybe on another planet, or another galaxy. You never ever want to show your face again.

    f. Wow! You weren't expecting to flat-out bomb, but it's cool. It doesn't bother you much.

# Answer: Let's Break It Down

If you answered **A**, **B**, **C**, or **E**, then JOIN THE CLUB. That's how most people feel about completely screwing up. Horrible. Physically sick. Anxious. Worried. In denial.

If you answered **D** or **F**, then you've started to figure out the secret to failure. By harnessing your thoughts and trying to see the big picture, you can cope with whatever happens. Once you've done that a bunch of times, you get braver, more confident, and willing to take more risks.

Maybe try thinking about it like this: if you aren't doing some failing, then you're not learning, you're not growing or becoming stronger, and you're likely not taking those important risks. You're also not creating fun and adventure for yourself. You probably don't have to think hard to remember moments when you've really learned from failure.

Failure will happen. The key isn't to avoid it. You can't. The key is knowing what to do with it. And we all need a cheat sheet to failure. Here's how to cope and grow:

# TOP TEN FAILURE FIXES

1. **BE YOUR OWN BFF.** Or, at the very least, be nice to yourself. Remind yourself that humans fail. It's a design flaw in the species. Let yourself wallow a bit if that helps and indulge in whatever makes you happier. Ice cream is good. Or ask for a hug.

2. **CHANGE THE CHANNEL.** What helps get your brain to a better place? Read a book. Watch TV. Listen to music. Hang out with a friend. Cuddle with your cat. Kick a ball. Figure out a way to distract yourself from what's just happened. There's no need to turn it over and over in your mind.

3. **PUT IT IN PERSPECTIVE.** Think back to similar situations and remind yourself that you survived! Reassure yourself that usually people aren't talking about you, snickering about you, or staring at you when you fail. Are you constantly thinking of the time your friend tripped and spilled milk on the older kids' table in the cafeteria? Did you dump her? Unlikely.

4. **ASK FOR HELP.** Science shows that one of the best ways to get past failure is to open up and share what happened to you. Talk to your parents, your friends, your favorite teacher, or your guidance counselor.

5. **MIND YOUR MINDSET.** Try to think *setback* instead of *failure*, and view that setback as temporary, not permanent. It's a problem to be solved, not a life sentence. Ask yourself, "What did I learn? What will I do next time? What will I totally NOT do?"

6. **RELY ON ROLE MODELS.** Remember that list of role models you started? Dig around for cool failure stories and add them. Everybody who's anybody has failed. Put your own name there. List one of your own epic fails, including the strategy for getting over it.

7. **THINK SMALL.** Similar to how you might handle a risk, break the reasons for your failure down into smaller chunks that are easier to handle and then tackle those chunks one at a time

8. **REPEAT, REPEAT, REPEAT.** A bit of practice, doing things over and over, makes them easier—and helps protect against nerves. Ever

heard of muscle memory? That's when your muscles go through the motions while your brain is distracted. That's a good thing!

9. **DIVE BACK IN.** As soon as you're ready, dust yourself off and stare at the failure straight in the face. Take another whack at it, determined not to make that same mistake again. Other mistakes, well, yeah. But not that exact same one.

10. **THE IT-COULD-BE-WORSE-MUCH-WORSE LIST.** This one's essential. You've got to keep your sense of humor when disaster strikes. Thoughts like "at least I didn't forget to put on pants and go to school naked after our roof caved in," or "at least my family wasn't featured on *The World's Biggest Dorks*," or "at least I didn't send a totally awkward message to the whole grade" can help remind you that it REALLY COULD BE WORSE!

As you can see, there're a lot of ways to reboot after failure. Check out these stories about Maria, Nell, and Lizbeth, who fall into the black pit of failure in mortifying, never-want-to-go-there ways. Think about which escape route you like better.

*Maria is excited about making friends with a new group of girls. She has a reputation for being sassy and funny, so she thinks that's how she'll cement her place.*

*In the midst of a group chat, she messages Carmen,*

*the one girl she MOST wants to impress, making*
*fun of what their friend Ashley wore to school that*
*day. "Maybe THAT'S why she's not invited to Ben's*
*party. Lol." She means to be funny, but it's also a little*
*mean. Then her phone blows up. She sent the message*
*not only to Carmen, but to THE WHOLE GROUP*
*TEXT. Now EVERYONE is mad at Maria and she*
*feels like they all hate her.*

**REBOOT OPTION 1:** Maria is freaking out, so she decides to create a calm space. She turns her phone off (#2, **Change the Channel**). She does beat herself up for a while and imagines she's doomed to a lonely life of no friends. But then she starts to remember that other people mess up all the time, on- and offline (#3, **Put It in Perspective**) and they do not end up as outcasts.

**REBOOT OPTION 2:** Maria is so mad at herself. She decides to kick a ball with her brother for a while. She knows that will make her feel better (#2, **Change the Channel**). Then what? She decides to figure out what to do next. There's clearly a solution (#5, **Mind Your Mindset**). Her goal is still to be friends with Carmen and Ashley. To do that, she takes it one step at a time (#7, **Think Small**). First up: apologies! She'll tell Ashley how sorry she is, really and truly. She talks to Ashley, and then she talks to Carmen (#9, **Dive Back In**). It's pretty awkward . . . but a few weeks later things are back to normal.

*Nell does great in school, especially in English and social studies. She really wants to nail math and be in the advanced class. She works with a tutor, sits with her mom doing drills, and gets pumped for the placement test.*

*But when the test is in front of her, Nell's chest feels like someone is trying to wring out all the air. She cannot move her hand and she's barely breathing. When the teacher asks if she needs help, she cannot even use words. She just shakes her head, hands him the blank page, and walks out the door. Everyone saw her, everyone knows. She bombed. Totally bombed.*

**REBOOT OPTION 1:** When Nell gets home, she lounges in her room, watching Harry Potter movies and eating kettle corn. Cries a couple of times, but tells herself it's OK (#1, **Be Your Own BFF**). It's hard to stop thinking about what this means: she's so dumb that nobody will like her . . . she'll never go to high school . . . she'll wind up jobless and homeless . . . until she says to herself, "KNOCK IT OFF!" She tells herself that none of those things will happen, then she deliberately asks her mom, who is one of her heroes, for help (#4, **Ask for Help**). Her mom describes failing her driving test—three times. Nell chuckles and feels better (#6, **Rely on Role Models**).

**REBOOT OPTION 2:** Nell tries to calm down, but this test disaster keeps bugging her. She feels like there's only one thing to do: keep on pushing—do something about it. First things first (#5, **Mind Your Mindset**). She decides to go back over the practice tests and see what went wrong. Looking them over, she realizes that she can totally do the work: that was not the problem. Panic was the problem. She needs to take it step by step (#7, **Think Small**). Instead of getting hit with the weight of the WHOLE TEST at once, she could have just taken it in slowly, one question at a time. She wants to be ready for the next opportunity and emails her teacher about when she can try to get into that advanced class again.

*Lizbeth is a great soccer player. As goalie, she gets to direct everyone throughout the game, placing them exactly the way she wants, so that she can keep track of the ball.*

*In the final game of the season, she's in the zone,*

*calling plays and passes with perfect accuracy. Then, out of nowhere, the ball zips toward her. Her teammates rush to defend the goal, but she calls out MINE MINE MINE. She leaps toward the ball, ready to scoop it up midair, and save the day as usual. WHOOSH. It hits the net behind her. A goal for the other team. Game OVER, and she lost it. All her teammates groan and crumple in defeat, and Lizbeth knows that she cost them the game.*

**REBOOT OPTION 1:** Lizbeth just wants to be alone. She won't talk to her teammates or her parents and runs straight to her room when she gets home, sobbing. But then she remembers something that helped last time she was upset. She grabs a book and gets her mind to another place (#1, **Be Your Own BFF**, and #2, **Change the Channel**). By dinner, she tells her mother that she remembers when she let a key shot get by in a different game—right into the corner—and how she learned to block better because of it (#3, **Put It in Perspective**). She decides to ask her coach about working with her a little more (#8, **REPEAT, REPEAT, REPEAT**)—and she moves on.

**REBOOT OPTION 2:** Lizbeth rushes to apologize to her teammates and they hug her, chiming in with mistakes they've all made. The whole group hug turns into a memory-fest of screw-ups, with their coach jumping right in. Then they all shout out all the things that could have really gone completely awry (#10, **It-Could-Be-Worse-Much-Worse List).** What if Lizbeth had broken her leg? What if a tornado struck the field? What if there had been a zombie apocalypse? They all laugh. For Lizbeth, that miss is going to loom large for a while. But her team will play again next week (#9, **Dive Back In**). Getting back on that field is the best thing for her, because she will get swept up and not have much time to dwell.

## WHEN FAILURE STRIKES HARD

In "Kayla's Big Risk," not making the team strikes her as the most humiliating fail ever. But, in fact, you'll see that she discovers it was just a setback, and her attitude about it leads her to great places.

Still, some failures do seem almost too much to bear. Remember Helen, the girl at the start of the chapter who froze solid on stage? She spent *a lot of time* thinking she was a loser. Failure itself can absolutely get etched in your brain, especially if you don't take a hold of it. Sometimes you will need to **change that channel** *constantly*—even use the whole cheat sheet—and still it might take a *long* time.

Helen ended up back on stage, if you can believe it. Helen's parents helped her by continuing to point out acting opportunities. Finally, Helen started doing small roles at school before eventually applying to a performing arts high school. She got in! She *still* gets super anxious before she goes on stage, but the repetition helps. It often calms her down to remind herself that she's already experienced the worst failure ever—and she survived! And she's still flubbing lines here and there, and building confidence.

## Use This Handy-Dandy Remote to Change the Channel in Your Brain

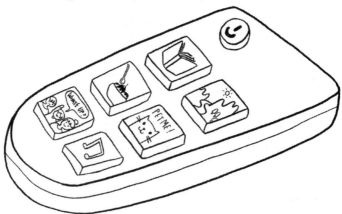

# KAYLA'S BIG RISK, PART 2

# GIRLS OF ACTION

Sixteen-year-old Olivia Lee is the head of the gay-straight alliance at her school. Olivia is Korean American and has never felt that she fits the typical stereotype of Asian girls. People often assume that Asian girls are quiet, hardworking, excellent students, particularly in math, and a little shy, even dainty. Olivia is very bold and assertive. Sometimes people have given her a hard time about being different, which used to hurt her feelings.

Olivia decided to start an empowerment club for Asian girls in the middle school that's attached to her high school. She wanted it to be a place where they could be open, be rowdy, or complain about parents and homework. She made presentations to tell the girls all about it. But in the end, not a single girl signed up. Not one. At first she was upset. But then, after a while, when Olivia broke things down in her mind, she started to realize that, in her excitement, she probably talked more than she listened, and also failed to show them how powerful this club could be. She's working on a more inclusive message that emphasizes her belief that nobody needs to fit a stereotype.

"We are all enough," Olivia says.

Instead of thinking of it as a giant, overwhelming disaster, and giving up, she realized she could start to plan for next year, and try it again with what she learned. It may have been a failure the first time, but she's determined to turn that failure into fuel to help younger girls.

# CHAPTER 4

## BECOME A CULTURE CRITIC

## CONFIDENCE CLOSE-UP

Della couldn't wait to get to the huge new sporting-goods store. As she started looking for things to try on, she gravitated to the boys' section—her typical move. She wasn't into pink or purple sports gear or short shorts like a lot of other girls. Then Della started noticing the gigantic shots of athletes on the walls. Sick! But wait ... The boys in the photos were all in action poses: shooting, dribbling, throwing, jumping, sweating. The girls, on the other hand, were just ... posing. One had her hand on her hip, looking like she was flirting with the camera. A few girls were running, but just playing around—no sweating, no intensity. Della felt that familiar sense of frustration, and a kind of shrinking. She tried to shrug it off, found some cool gear, and moved on to shoes.

Della didn't think she'd ever seen so many basketball shoes. Flashy, plain, Velcro, laces, shiny, multicolored—awesome! Her feet were big enough for women's shoes, but not quite big enough for men's, and when she asked where to look for the women's selections, she was told something shocking. ALL of the shoes on the floor were for MEN, or kids. Turns out the store didn't stock any women's basketball shoes; those shoes were only online. At first, Della thought it was a joke. Then red fury washed through her brain. What the ... "What's the matter with these people? What do they think about girls and women? Don't they get that we're playing, too?"

Have you ever had an experience like that? Or noticed something about the way the world views

## Fair Play!

In 1972, a revolutionary law called Title IX (or nine, for those of us not living in ancient Rome) made it illegal to spend more money on boys' sports in public schools and universities than on girls'. Before Title IX, girls had fewer school teams and far fewer players. Sometimes they didn't even have balls or uniforms. There were only three hundred thousand girls in the whole country playing sports in high school and college. Today, more than forty years later, there are well over three million. People noticed that girls didn't have the same options and, even though it wasn't easy, they finally changed that by passing this law. What a difference! And there's more. Today, girls who play team sports are more likely to graduate from college and work in the male-dominated areas that tend to make more money. They're usually more resilient and more open to the experience of trying and failing, winning and losing. But girls still drop out of sports more often than boys do during adolescence, when worry and self-consciousness can be overwhelming. Please, don't quit! Sticking with it matters.

women and girls that seems kind of unfair? People treating you differently because you're a girl? (Maybe sometimes you're treated better. Teachers tend to favor girls because they are less likely to be troublemakers, and often perform better in school. Back to that later.) You may not have ever shopped for basketball shoes, but you can probably understand how wrong Della's experience feels.

# THE POWER OF OBSERVATION

Part of your ability to feel confident doesn't come from inside of you. It comes from the way the world works and how that affects you. Sometimes you can change the culture. But the most important thing to do is NOTICE it. We've been using the word *notice* a lot, because it's a critical confidence skill. When you turn your gaze at the world, being able to *notice* will help you understand that the feelings you're having aren't random, that you're not alone in having them, and that you might even be able to take positive action. Becoming a culture critic puts the power back in your hands.

With Della, for example, at that athletic store, she knew that her feelings of frustration weren't wrong or silly. The problem wasn't her; the problem was the store, and the culture that made it seem fine to decorate and stock a store in such an unbalanced way. She deserves shoes to try on. And now, she can decide whether to do something about it—like post something on social media or write a letter to the CEO.

## CONFIDENCE WARM-UP

Look around. These are things some of the girls we talked to noticed. Whether or not they frustrate you personally, think about them for a minute.

- Girls, more often than boys, are called "bossy" or "pushy" or "obnoxious" when they speak up or take a stand.
- Girls get more clothes, or headbands, or stuffed animals for birthdays or holidays. Boys get more games and balls.
- Toy stores usually separate toys into boy and girl sections. Girls have more dolls on their shelves; boys have more things to build. The girl sections are seas of pink.
- The universal image for a woman on bathroom signs is a cutout figure of a girl in a skirt.
- Teachers or coaches make jokes like "Boys will be boys."

 **QUIZ**

**Here's a pretty normal situation, yet . . . there's something off about it.**

*Gigi gets hooked on a new medical drama. There's a team of four doctors: two men, Dr. Scott and Dr. Gregory, and two women, Dr. Runner and Dr.*

*Hernandez. It's all about a scary medical mystery. Dr. Scott and Dr. Gregory end up having a huge argument about it, nearly killing their patient. At the last minute, they discover the cure. Dr. Runner totally has a crush on Dr. Scott and gets lots of hilarious advice from Dr. Hernandez.*

## What's wrong with this picture?

Two male and two female doctors. All good. Right? Wrong. Because what's the actual story about? For women, it's about romance. For men, it's about work. If you noticed that, good eye!

## YES, THESE THINGS ACTUALLY HAPPENED!

◆ In 2016, the September issues of *Boys' Life* and *Girls' Life* magazines looked wildly different. The cover of the boys' magazine had headlines like "exploring your future" and "here's how to be what you want to be" and offered career options like astronaut and firefighter. The girls' magazine cover promised the lowdown on "dream hair," how to "wake up pretty," "friendship rules," "my first kiss," and "the new denim checklist."

◊ Target introduced a new girls' T-shirt with a Batgirl to-do list on the front. It was pink and proclaimed: "Dryclean cape, wash Batmobile, fight crime, save the world." In that order.

◊ In 2016, Gap ran an ad with a photo of a boy and a girl. The little boy was wearing a T-shirt with a picture of Albert Einstein on it, and the text in the ad read "little scholar." The girl wore a sweater with the letter *G* on it, accompanied by the text "social butterfly" and "talk of the playground."

## LIKE A GIRL

You must have heard some of these:

✮ Don't be such a girl.

✮ You throw like a girl.

✮ You play like a girl.

✮ Don't cry like a girl.

✮ You squeal like a girl.

✮ You run like a girl.

 **QUIZ**

**When people add "like a girl" after any verb, is that:**

a. Something thoughtful, meant to let everyone know how strong and powerful girls are?

b. Something closer to an insult, implying that doing something in a girl way is lame?

## Answer: Let's Break It Down

We think you know which answer is true.

Girls are strong and powerful, as good as (and often even better than) boys at all kinds of stuff. But there are some old-fashioned assumptions out there that girls are somehow weaker, or less competitive, or sillier.

In the last few years, though, people really started to notice those particular words. And they decided to do something about it. They reclaimed the phrase and made it awesome. Check out the hashtag **#likeagirl** and see what it means now!

Start to look around you for clues about how girls and women are treated differently. You don't have

to be defined by anybody else's version of what you
should be.

## CONFIDENCE CLOSE-UP

In seventh grade, Jamie was supposed to write
a paper on something she was passionate about.
She chose to focus on abuse toward women.
It's an upsetting subject, but she believed it
was necessary to shine a light on it. When Jamie
brought her presentation to school, her teacher
refused to accept it. Even though other kids in
the class focused on graphic, violent subjects like
animal abuse, genocide, or cannibalism, Jamie's
concept was considered "inappropriate" because it
was too "advanced." Also, some of the teachers were
concerned that it would come across as "offensive"
to her male classmates. So she had to start
over. And this wasn't an isolated incident: Jamie
is constantly harassed at school for her strong
opinions—and all the name-calling has to do with
her being a girl.

## CONFIDENCE WARM-UP

Let's start to hone your powers of observation. Think about the following scenarios, discuss them over lunch with your friends, or pull out your phone and start a group chat.

- In action movies, who usually has all the cool battles and adventures? What are the girls/women doing? What are the boys/men doing?

- If you have brothers, what kinds of chores do they do? What kinds of chores do you do?

- When you meet friends of your parents, do you get more compliments on how you look and how cute your outfit is? Or on something you're good at doing or something you've done?

- At kids' birthday parties, are there different kinds of themes for girls and boys?

- Next time you're at the doctor's office, flip through a sports magazine. Count how many male athletes you see. Now count the female athletes.

- Flip through a news magazine. How many articles are about things men have done, or male leaders? Now, what about women?
- Do you ever consider whether something is appropriate for you because you are a girl?

Life isn't always fair. The playing field isn't always level for everyone at every moment. But if you become a culture critic, you'll have the power of knowing it's not all your fault, and it might spur you to action!

## GIRLS IN THE WORLD

Here are some stories we've heard about things girls have noticed. Once you start to look around, it gets easier to develop your own voice and start forming your own opinions.

*Eleven-year-old Ellie is careful about raising her hand. She thinks about her answer before sticking her hand up. She wants to make sure she has something valuable to say. But the boys in her class tend to wave their hands madly or call out whatever pops into their* heads, even when it means they're talking over her or someone else. Sometimes the teacher tells them to wait their turn, but plenty of times she chuckles as though it's beyond her control and uses their shouted-out comments to help guide the conversation. And then Ellie feels stupid sitting there with her hand up, following the rules.

## What did Ellie notice?

For Ellie, it seems like there are different standards for girls and boys. She hears the rules and follows them, meanwhile some boys don't pay as much attention to what they're "supposed to do." Next time she might say, "Hey, *I'm* talking!" if she's interrupted, or keep waving her hand until she gets to speak.

*Patricia plays basketball in a bunch of different leagues. At practice one night, the coach told her team to grab a seat on the bleachers because they had special guests, representatives from some major sporting-goods clothing brands. One was a former pro ball player! Patricia was so excited to hear about what it's like to be at the top of your game and playing in big arenas, and maybe to get some tips for a winning mindset. Instead,* the sports rep and the player gave a talk about how to look your best while playing ball, and showed samples of stylish sports clothes and waterproof makeup.

## What did Patricia notice?

For Patricia, *playing* her best matters more than *looking* her best. She doesn't really care about how cool her gear is, just whether she can win. It felt like she was being told that how she looked was as important as how she played, and that was upsetting to her. Do boys get tips on looking cute while they play competitive sports?

*Dress codes are SUCH a big problem for lots of girls, including thirteen-year-old Cammie. She's been "dress coded" and given a detention slip for wearing high-waisted jeans and a crop top (when she bends over, her back shows), for sporting leggings, and for letting her bra straps show when she wore a tank top on a hot day. Yet boys walk around school with their underwear showing above their saggy jeans all the time. The code for girls is more enforced because the school does not want boys "distracted."*

## What did Cammie notice?

For Cammie, the dress code doesn't feel fair—she thinks the girls are being held to a tougher standard than boys. What do you think?

### CONFIDENCE WARM-UP

Take out your phone, or borrow one from your parents. Girls all over the world use TONS of emojis every day—like, over a million, actually. Take a look: are the emojis capturing all the great stuff girls do? Recently, people started to notice that the emojis for girls were pretty lame: princesses, brides, dancers, girls with kitty ears.

## EMOJI-ISM

GIRLS CLAMORED FOR BETTER EMOJIS!

That inspired a push to have emojis of girls DOING all kinds of things. What do you see on your screen? Are you and your friends represented there?

## STEREOTYPING

This is a useful word to know. You probably hear it tossed around a lot. It's when assumptions that are way too simple, and often wrong, are made about a particular group of people. It happens for a reason. It's kind of easy, and sometimes it can feel comfortable to put people into a group based on looks, race, ethnicity, nationality, profession, hair color, gender—almost anything—and believe they are similar. But whenever we assume that people in any group are all alike, it can lead to trouble. All girls aren't alike, all boys aren't alike, all teachers aren't alike, all parents . . . See where we're going with this?

Stereotyping can do a lot of harm. It can shove you *in* an uncomfortable box, or keep you *out* of the place you think you belong. That's what happened to Zena.

## CONFIDENCE CLOSE-UP

For her senior yearbook picture, Zena wore a tuxedo that she got from a thrift store. She thought she totally rocked it. When she arrived at the gym for her photo appointment, the photographer looked worried and called the guidance counselor over. The counselor told her that she would have to go home and change. Apparently, the tuxedo was considered "not ladylike," so she was not allowed to wear it. The counselor also muttered something about it not being fair to the other kids for her to look so weird in the yearbook. In the end, Zena had to go home and find a dress.

## CONFIDENCE WARM-UP

What do you see in your own family?

◊ Do people treat your mom and dad differently because of their different genders?

- ◊ Do mechanics talk more to your dad than your mom?
- ◊ If you live in a single-parent household, maybe you've noticed that nobody thinks your dad can cook, or maybe nobody thinks your mom can fix a leak.
- ◊ When you are out to eat with adults, who gets the bill?
- ◊ If you have brothers, do people ask them different kinds of questions than they ask you?

Maya told us that even parents with the best intentions can sometimes have "higher" and more stressful expectations for girls.

## CONFIDENCE CLOSE-UP

Maya, a twenty-year-old college student, remembers that her parents always expected her to do very different things from her brothers. "As a teenager, I was lucky enough to have parents who let me be independent. In many ways, it was great! I discovered that the more you show you can do things for yourself, the more others assume you can do those things. I became a great cook, for example. Unfortunately, this eventually became a bit of a problem. When you always get As, no one is impressed if you get another one, right? Since I was able to help look after my little sister, my parents began to assume that I would always make time to babysit her, and help my brother with his homework, and do some of the cooking. At the beginning, it was fine. But after a while it became stressful always having to look after others before starting on my own homework or going out with my friends. The more I helped, the more my parents asked me to do, and the more they talked about how great it was that their daughter was 'so reliable' and 'so helpful.' I started to feel that my parents' opinion of me was dependent on me always being 'so helpful.'

"Now I realize that I could have told them I was overwhelmed. After all, both my brothers said no all the time. But I never felt that I could do that. I'd love to go back and tell my teenage self that being able to stand up for your own happiness isn't selfish or weak but is actually a pretty strong thing to do."

# WOMEN IN THE WORLD

It's important to look at the adult world with a critical eye as well. In the last few years, the whole world is paying a lot more attention to culture and how women are treated. Here are some facts to get you started.

## You should know:

- ✮ Girls do better than boys in school at all ages and subjects.
- ✮ Countries with more gender equity are wealthier and healthier.
- ✮ Businesses with more female leaders make more money.
- ✮ Female members of Congress are more effective lawmakers because they pass more legislation and work with opponents more often.

## You should ALSO know:

- ✮ As of October 2017, only eleven heads of state

and twelve heads of government were women, out of almost 200 countries.

✮ Only 25 percent of jobs in science, technology, engineering, and math (STEM) in the US are held by women.

✮ Women earn about 83 percent of what men earn, no matter what they do for a living. So when most men make a dollar, women make eighty-three cents doing the same job.

✮ In the entire US Congress (the House of Representatives and the Senate), there are 535 members. Currently, just 105 are women.

## But the public is starting to notice:

✮ Recently, one of the few women in the Senate was publicly shushed twice by one of her male colleagues while she was questioning the US deputy attorney general (also a male). Many in the public were outraged, the media covered it, and women all over the country came out with similar stories of being shushed by men.

✮ Another female senator was literally silenced

on the floor of the Senate as she tried to read
an historic letter. Women everywhere got really
mad. The story inspired a children's book.

✶ A top female physicist was the only woman
on a panel at the World Science Festival. The
moderator kept interrupting her. An audience
member finally told him to knock it off. The
festival got more attention for the interrupting
than the science.

✶ A growing chorus of courageous women in all
sorts of jobs have been coming forward, often
risking their livelihoods, to talk openly about
mistreatment in the workplace.

Every day, women around the world are doing brave
things.

## CONFIDENCE IN ACTION

Major General Jessica Wright is one of the highest-
ranking women in the US military. Even though she
succeeds in a world of square-jawed generals and
majors—mostly male—she manages to be utterly
herself. And she kicks butt. She became the first

woman to command an army combat brigade. Yet she still remembers when she was a brand-new lieutenant and one of her superiors told her up front that he was not in favor of women in the military. Not at all. "There were five hundred things going through my head," she said. "And I looked at him, summoned my courage, and said, 'You have an opportunity now to get over that. Sir.'" It worked. She won his respect and her career soared.

We don't have all the answers, but we just want you to know that your confidence can get shaken by things that are out of your control. Talk to the women in your life: your mother, aunts, teachers, coaches, anyone. Ask them questions, so that you are armed with helpful information to make you stronger.

# GIRLS OF ACTION

Fourteen-year-old Shiloh Gonsky has been a baseball catcher for nine years. When she first started playing, there were plenty of girls on her travel baseball team. By the time she was twelve, there were only a handful. Now, she's the only girl catcher in her age bracket, one of only three girls playing at all in her division.

When she was little, Shiloh's gender did not matter. But as she got older, parents and other players started staring at her. She got lots of unwanted advice to switch to softball, like other girls. "I don't want to stop baseball—I love it. I don't want to play with a bigger, softer ball and a smaller field." Even in the batting cages at a serious spring training camp, she was aware of older kids staring and pointing. But she will not quit. She thinks playing baseball has given her the confidence to do a ton of stuff, but mostly she hopes that by sticking with it, she makes it more normal for others. "I don't want it to be surprising that a girl would play baseball. I want to prove myself worthy and show that a girl can play."

## PIECING TOGETHER THE CODE

The chapters you've just finished all point to the first piece of the code: *Risk More!*

1. Risk More!
2. _____
3. _____

We hope when you see those two simple words, they will remind you of all the reasons you need to be a Girl of Action. Risk is a major part of confidence building. You've got to try stuff, all kinds of stuff, even if you fail sometimes, so you start building up your confidence supply.

SECTION 2

# CONFIDENCE INSIDE & OUT

# ALEX VS. HER BRAIN, PART 1

## TO BE CONTINUED . . .

# CHAPTER 5

## YOU & YOUR BRAIN

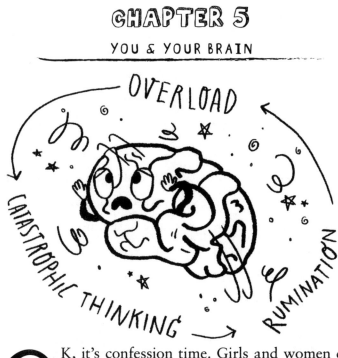

OK, it's confession time. Girls and women can overthink things. We all seem to worry too often that we've messed up or that everything is horrible. Like Alex in "Alex vs. Her Brain," you may have one small stressful thought that quickly blooms into absolute certainty that you're a misfit and everyone in the world is staring at you. Or maybe that particular thing doesn't upset you, but you worry your best friend just isn't as into you as she used to be, or you worry you let the whole cast in the school play down by missing an entrance cue.

Psychologists call that *ruminating*—when thoughts

go round and round in your head and you feel like a frantic hamster stuck on a wheel. We call it overthinking. You probably call it being trapped with the absolute WORST thoughts that will never ever go away. Either way, it stinks. Bad. Once those I'm-the-lamest-person-who-ever-lived thoughts get in your head, good luck trying to get them out. It's easy to see why ruminating is a confidence killer. Are you really in the mood for risky action when your brain is spinning like a top?

Just for "fun," let's take a ride in an out-of-control brain—maybe it'll look familiar to you.

## CONFIDENCE CONUNDRUM:
### Academic Armageddon

You get a bad grade on your end-of-semester test that you studied so hard for, covering material you thought you understood perfectly. And, even worse, all your friends did well. Failing this test, you are certain, is worse than a meteorite destroying the earth.

Let's go through this scenario properly and experience the agony for a hot moment. Hey, at least we're doing it together!

Your teacher passes out the graded tests. Other kids look pleased, including the girl you studied with. OK, that's a great sign. Then he puts your test down in front of you. Emblazoned at the top is a giant, pulsing, billboard-sized letter: D. Here's what's happening in your head:

*OMG. I spent hours studying for this test. OK. Hold it together. Are those tears I feel in the corners of my eyes? NO WAY. No crying. Please, please, please. Not now. Stop, tears, NOW. Did*

*the whole room suddenly go quiet? Noise,*
*chatter, anything—I need to hear something*
*besides the sound of my own failure. Will someone*
*please get yelled at so I don't have to sit here with*
*the WHOLE class staring at me?*

**When you're upset about a grade, you can
descend into a downward spiral at a dizzying
speed. You know how it goes:** *Everyone thinks I'm
a failure. . . . My teacher thinks I'm a failure. . . .
My friends think I'm a failure. . . . I'm a total
failure. . . . I will never get into a good school, I
might not even pass middle school. . . . My mom
is going to kill me. . . . Maybe I'm just dumb. . . . I
will always just be totally stupid at math.*

**How long do these thoughts go on?**

20 minutes?

1 hour?

6 hours?

1 day?

3 days?

1 week?

2 weeks?

If you're beating yourself up about a bad grade for more than a day, that's exhausting. How many "I'm useless" thoughts have you let creep into your head? Five hundred? Two thousand? A gazillion? Are they making themselves right at home, having a great time in your brain, settling right in and stretching out?

Yup. That's ruminating for you.

The good news: We can stop it. But first, we need to take a closer look at it.

# EXPEDITION INTO YOUR BRAIN

What's going on in that massive organ living in our skull? It's an amazing control center. But it can also crank out some pretty crazy ways of thinking. This is where your *noticing skills* become especially valuable again. Turn them inward. When we observe our thoughts, we can actually change them.

Just to be clear—we're not telling you to think more, or add to the ruminating! *Observing* your thoughts is a skill scientists call **metacognition**. It's like watching your thoughts and feelings *from a distance*. Ruminating is like being stuck *inside* the terrifying tornado of those thoughts.

Check out the most common flawed thinking patterns. Do they sound like you?

**CATASTROPHIC:** Do you jump to the WORST conclusions? Imagine disaster around every corner? In your world, are people never late—they're always dead? Does the bad always seem more powerful than the good? Does getting one bad grade, like in our Academic Armageddon scenario, mean more bad grades will surely follow?

**MIND READER:** Do you assume that you know what other people are thinking—especially when it's about you? Like, you're SURE that everyone in class saw you burst into a Noah's Ark–level flood of tears? Are you pretty sure that anything bad happening is basically about YOU, or that people think so? If two people are whispering in class, it MUST be about your stupid answer? Or about what you're wearing?

**SET IN STONE:** Do you feel like things just are what they are—fixed in place? Like there's no way to make changes? That grade on the essay clearly means you're dumb, and there's not much to do about it. It had nothing to do with effort, or understanding the project—you're just bad at school. Or when you miss a backhand in tennis, do you automatically think, "I'm bad at tennis," versus, "I'm bad at backhands—I need to work on them"?

The headline is: **we basically lie to ourselves—a lot.** Being a **catastrophic, mind reading,** or **set in stone** thinker means you are telling yourself wilder tall tales than any fib you'd ever try on a parent or friend. *Notice these lies your brain tells you and how painful they can be.*

Here's why the messed-up thinking can do real damage:

what we THINK creates what we FEEL, which then shapes what we DO.

And that's where all this ties into confidence. Too much thinking—or, more accurately, too much flawed thinking—leads to bad feelings, and sometimes reckless action. But most often, it leads to NO ACTION. We become paralyzed, or frightened. And no action means no confidence building.

### CONFIDENCE WARM-UP

Check out how a different way of *thinking* about the exact same situation can directly shape your *feelings*, and then your *actions*.

## Scenario #1

**Situation:** Eleven-year-old Zo works hard to prepare to perform a traditional Indian dance at a family party.

↓

**Thoughts:** "What if I do it all wrong and disappoint my family? What if I ruin the whole celebration? So many things could go wrong."

↓

**Feelings:** Nervous, worried, anxious

↓

**Action:** Zo tells her mom she's just way too nervous and bows out. Then, at the party, she's frustrated to see her cousin up there performing, when it could have been her.

## Scenario #2

**Situation:** Eleven-year-old Zo works hard to prepare to perform a traditional Indian dance at a family party.

↓

**Thoughts:** "It's so cool that my parents finally asked me to take part in a family tradition and I'll get to show off all my hard work! It might not be perfect, and I'm nervous, but it's in front of family members who love and support me."

↓

**Feelings:** Excited, pleased, proud

↓

**Action:** Zo carries it off with one or two mistakes, but is proud of herself and gets wild applause.

## Scenario #1

**Situation:** Keisha is an excellent baker, and her teacher asks her to make something special for the bake sale to fund a class trip to Six Flags.

↓

**Thoughts:** "What if everyone hates my muffins? What if they're dry and look lumpy? If they don't sell, it'll be all my fault that we don't get to go on the trip."

↓

**Feelings:** Nervous, anxious, worried

↓

**Action:** Scattered attention, which means one batch ends up getting burned

## Scenario #2

**Situation:** Keisha is an excellent baker, and her teacher asks her to make something special for the bake sale to fund a class trip to Six Flags.

↓

**Thoughts:** "It makes me feel good that my teacher asked me to take this on. She must have faith in me. My friends love what I bake!"

↓

**Feelings:** Proud, satisfied, competent

↓

**Action:** A smooth evening of baking, with time to watch TV

See what a difference it makes if you can corral those wild thoughts?

## YOUR TURN

Try this:

Sit in a comfortable position and close your eyes. Remember something bad that happened to you, or something you thought was awful: a terrible grade, a mean comment from a friend, a fight with your parents or a sibling, or something worse we can't imagine. Spend some time with those negative thoughts. Set them loose in your head. *Do you notice how, just remembering them, you FEEL sad or angry or really, really down?*

Now, try to remember something wonderful. A

great time with your puppy, an amazing comment from a teacher on your paper, a win with your team, or time with a good friend. Try to relive that moment in your head. *Notice how you may even be smiling, and feel calmer and more upbeat?*

You generated both sets of feelings by putting those specific thoughts in your head. You can see why we need to keep track of our mind games.

## CONFIDENCE WARM-UP

Start to notice that boys and girls sometimes have very different thoughts about the same situation. Here's a tale of two brains.

*Ciara was working on a group project in science and thought she had a great idea for the electrical board they were making. She told the other kids about it, and then Leo said, "Hey, not sure **that** will work, but if we try it **and** add tinfoil to conduct the electricity, then it will totally rock!"*

| Ciara's Thoughts | Leo's Thoughts |
|---|---|
| Ciara's feelings were hurt. She worries that now her group mates all believe that she's the girl with stupid ideas. And, obviously, Leo thinks she's an idiot, right? | Leo doesn't think anything's wrong. He didn't shoot down her whole idea, he just made a suggestion to make it work better. In Leo's mind, they were working well together. |

# IT'S ALL IN YOUR HEAD

Girls are great at assuming we're wrong. To prove it, here's a scientific experiment that's been repeated over and over, with the same results. College students were about to take a pop quiz in science. Beforehand, they were asked to predict how they'd do. Boys thought they'd get about 7 out of 10 right, girls estimated 5.8 out of 10. Then they took the test. After the test, the students were asked how they did. The boys guessed they did better than they actually did. The girls guessed they did much worse. Turns out, they all scored about the same, with both boys and girls getting around 7 out of 10. But the girls assumed the worst. Have you ever had that happen about a test, or something else? Often, we just don't believe that we are as awesome as we are. What's going on?

## BRAIN FACTOIDS

Are male and female brains different? We were obsessed with this question in our adult book. In the big picture: men and women, girls and boys, have the same basic intelligence. But there are some functional differences. Keep in mind, these differences aren't black and white, and they don't apply to everyone, but they're common enough to make them worth thinking about.

♦ Girls' and women's brains tend to have a more active prefrontal cortex—that area behind your forehead. That's where reason lives. Scientists think that could be why girls tend to be great big-picture thinkers and problem solvers.

♦ Girls usually have stronger emotional links to our memories because of a more developed hippocampus, the part of the brain where memories are stored. Boys remember as much, but often without the layer of emotion.

♦ Girls are way better at multitasking than boys, because we are more likely to use both hemispheres of the brain all the time. Boys have a tendency to rely on just the left side, which emphasizes thinking deeply about one thing.

♦ Girls tend to have higher emotional intelligence (called EQ) than boys. Our limbic system, the emotional control center of the brain, is larger and more developed. This gives us the ability to read other people's expressions and emotions well.

♦ There's a part of all brains scientists call the worrywart center. (Actually, it's the anterior cingulate gyrus. No wonder it has a nickname!) The worrywart center, which is good at spotting problems, is bigger in female brains.

♦ Scientists have found that more neurons are firing at any given moment in the brains of girls and women. Our brains appear to be doing more all the time.

# How Your Brain Works

Lots of these things are amazing. The female brain is powerful, and it gives us a lot of advantages. But—here's the way we like to think about it—we run into problems when we use too much of a great thing. Our very active and capable brains sometimes encourage us to worry, to overthink, to chew on memories. And we imagine crazy consequences. Then we end up being more cautious, taking fewer risks, being more stressed, and having WAY less fun.

## CONFIDENCE CLOSE-UP

Luna has a lot of stories about overthinking. So many that it was hard for her to pick just one! One time, her math teacher insisted she make up a test she missed when she was sick the day before. She begged for more time to prepare, but he wasn't having it. Math is her best subject and her teacher believed she was ready. Instead of just taking a deep breath and getting on with it, her thoughts were ZOOMING all over and she was almost paralyzed. She grasped at a crazy notion—to deliberately fail. Her teacher had a policy that students who failed could retake the test. So, she tried scrambling to figure out the right answer and then erasing it and putting another in its place. Her teacher realized what she was doing and stopped her. Holding the paper up to the light, he could see her original answers and gave her partial credit, a C. The lowest grade she'd ever gotten. If she could have squashed that overthinking, she would have done much better.

If any of this sounds familiar, you're NOT nuts and you're NOT alone. Our brains can work this way, for both girls and grown women.

Since we're so good at predicting the future, let's look at the biggest consequence of overthinking when it comes to confidence: not jumping into life with both feet, not taking risks, NOT having all the adventures we could be having because a quicksand of worry and doubt freezes us.

## CONFIDENCE CLOSE-UP

For eleven-year-old June, sleepovers and school trips are scary. She tries hard to be as excited as other kids, but then her mind starts spinning in dizzying circles. Having fun? Impossible to imagine. She can't stop thinking about all the unknowns: what if she gets sick and her mom's not there? What if there's nothing for her to eat? What if the bathroom is far away? What if she gets scared or homesick? If she's staying at her friend's house, maybe that would be better—at least her parents could get there fast. But a school trip overnight? What if she gets carsick? What if they get lost on the bus? Just thinking about it gives her a stomachache. June winds up saying NO to fun opportunities and staying home a lot of times because her scared and negative thoughts crowd out everything else.

# REWIRING: CHANGE YOUR BRAIN

Our brains may veer toward some faulty thinking patterns, but here's one of the coolest things about them: we can make new highways and byways in our brains any time we want. Cutting-edge scientists have discovered that the brain can actually be rewired by thinking about and doing things differently, and by forming new habits. They call it *neuroplasticity*. We call it amazing.

That ability to rewire our brains is the basic biological reason we are even able to build more confidence for ourselves. Scientists have studied the process on lots of things besides confidence. Here's a creepy example. Picture that slightly menacing way spiders walk, or more like stalk, as they approach some poor, unsuspecting prey. Does that send a shiver down your spine? A fear of spiders (*arachnophobia*) is very common. Scientists wanted to see whether brains with that fear could be rewired. They took a group of people who were afraid of spiders, showed them pictures of spiders and brought out some real spiders, all while watching their brains with special equipment. They saw the fear center—the amygdala—light up. Then these same scared people went into a room where they learned facts, for example, that most spiders aren't really harmful or out to get them. And then they had to approach, and ultimately touch, one of the biggest, hairiest spiders on the planet: a tarantula.

After those sessions, the scientists did the brain scans again while showing the participants pictures and then the real thing. Guess what? The fear center of the brain no longer lit up nearly as much. But our old friend the prefrontal cortex—the part of the brain that's all about rational thought—was working overtime. So, in a mere two hours, new wiring had been created. That's how quickly you can make some incredible changes in the way you think and feel.

## REWIRING TOOLBOX

Here's a toolbox full of the best tactics to wire your brain for confidence. Lots of the girls we talked with say they are already using some of them.

**TELL YOURSELF THE "MAYBE" STORY.** This is the number one shortcut for building a bridge out of any negative spiral. Here's how it works.

Say you're caught in a spin cycle every bit as frightening as a close-up with a spider. You can't stop obsessing about how you messed up that oral presentation today. You stumbled over the facts, dropped your index cards, and got things out of order. You're sure all the kids in your class are snickering and vowing never to be on group projects with you again. The smug look you thought you saw on the face of that annoying girl (let's call her Fiona) is haunting you.

What to do:

Create a new story about what happened, maybe a few of them, and start every sentence with *maybe*.

"Maybe Fiona wasn't even looking smug."

"Maybe she was thinking about that disgusting pizza at lunch."

"Maybe _____" (You fill in the blank.)

Scientists have studied this technique and found that even if the "maybe" is not the best explanation, even if the story is kind of silly, it works.

"Maybe nobody was paying attention because everyone's focused on that cute new boy's mysterious tattoo."

It sounds crazy, but try it. Flipping the switch to a slightly different way of looking at what's bugging you will get you off that negative path. Basically, you are *getting perspective*, and *thinking flexibly*, two critical confidence skills.

**LIST PAST ACCOMPLISHMENTS AS WELL AS THINGS YOU'RE LOOKING FORWARD TO.** This activates your brain's pleasure centers and keeps the brain's fear centers calm. Josie told us she keeps a list like this—she calls it her "best book"—right next to her bed. She pulls it out when she feels useless, and it helps remind her of all the things she's good at and is excited about. Start one in your Confidence Notebook.

**LOOK AT POSITIVE IMAGES AND THINK POSITIVE THOUGHTS TO CHANGE YOUR MOOD.** Scientists found we release endorphins—a feel-good hormone—when we stare at positive images. And when we think positive thoughts, the same thing happens. Even for just a minute! Sarita keeps photos on her phone of pictures of women doing amazing things. When she's stressed, a quick look makes her happy!

**HIT THE PAUSE BUTTON.** When Ivy wants to blow up, she makes herself hit Pause. She does nothing for a few minutes, and forces herself to sit still and breathe deeply. Researchers have spent a lot of time studying people who pause, control their breathing, and also meditate, and have noticed their fear centers are much smaller.

**CHANGE THE CHANNEL.** You remember this tip. It's a great brain de-stresser. Aria switches the subject in her head by putting on music, walking her dog, or practicing violin. Changing the channel also keeps our amygdala from getting out of control.

**WRITE DOWN NEGATIVE THOUGHTS AND THEN RIP**

## Gratitude Attitude

We've talked a lot about negative thoughts in this chapter. Here's another great way to change the channel: use gratitude. Scientists have found that people who spend more time being grateful every day are happier and healthier. Take out your notebook or grab your phone, and list three things to be grateful for every day. They might be three things you did well or three nice things other people did. Or they might be things like a good meal or a comforting hug or a gorgeous tree you caught a glimpse of. Set a daily reminder on your phone or put the list where you will see it each morning, so you can plant those seeds in your head to crowd out the negative weeds.

**THEM UP OR THROW THEM AWAY.** Scientists have discovered this symbolic act actually gives us more positive feelings. Natalie writes her bad thoughts down with thick markers on construction paper and then tears them into tiny pieces. She might make a mess, but she sure feels better!

**RIDE IN A HOT AIR BALLOON.** Not for real, though that would be fun. But the science on this is cool. Your brain relaxes when you literally take the time to imagine yourself in the basket, rising slowly above the clouds. First focus on the sky, the fields, the colors you see. And then look down at whatever problem is making you crazy as if it belongs to someone else, and you are just observing it. Your brain is getting perspective. When you start to direct your brain to observe things, even in your mind, like the sky and colors around you, the amygdala (fear center) calms down, and the prefrontal cortex (rational command center) kicks back in. Stella likes to play this game with her mom sometimes. Recently, she used it to figure out how to choose between her best friend's bat mitzvah and her boyfriend's bar mitzvah, which were on the same day! Once she was out of the weeds and up in the air, she could see her *friend* really needed her support more.

**FIND A LUCKY CHARM.** Look for something small, some little object that fits in your hand, and carry it with you. Pull it out when your brain starts to hit overload. Think of three words to describe it and really focus on them. Presto—calm descends. Coming up with the three words triggers the language part of your brain to *start* working, which means, you guessed it, the fear center in the back of your brain can *stop* churning. So keep your eyes peeled for your lucky charm, like a paper clip or hair tie or a key or a polished rock, and keep it with you.

## REWIRING IN ACTION

## CONFIDENCE CONUNDRUM:
### Back to Academic Armageddon

Here's how you might put those rewiring tools to use. Remember that classroom meltdown we told you about at the start of this chapter? You got that disappointing grade on your test. You could stop the turmoil in your brain immediately by trying to **change the channel**. Quickly think about anything else: kittens, a trip to the mall, or even better, other things you've done well recently. Later, likely at home, you can **take that mental hot air balloon ride**. With your calmer view from the clouds, consider how you got the bad grade. You know a D isn't normal, so what happened? Maybe the concepts just didn't make sense to you. Or you might realize you didn't study enough. Think back over the days before the test and figure out how much time you really put in. Were you distracted by soccer, Snapchat, or staring out the window? Once that's clear, it's easier to put things in perspective and move on.

## CONFIDENCE CONUNDRUM:
### Serious Sleepover Stress

Let's see how well *you* can manage your brain now.

You find out your BFF, Tori, had a sleepover with your other friend Sonya, and NEITHER of them told you beforehand. They don't know you know—even though you've tried to give them opportunities to be honest and normal about it—and it's super awkward, and you're hurt.

This definitely feels horrible, and your mind is careening in all sorts of negative directions. First, see whether you can match the thoughts to the type of faulty thinking taking place in your brain.

### Flawed Thinking Patterns

- Set in Stone
- Catastrophic
- Mind Reader

## Thoughts

a. "It's over. I can't be friends with Tori or Sonya ever again. In fact, I can't ever be friends with ANYONE ever again. Not that I will ever come out of my room. This is the worst day of my life!"

b. "I know they were chuckling about ditching me the whole time and giggling about what a dork I am. Obviously, they are talking about me constantly and are MASSIVELY over me."

c. "Nothing to do about it now, what's done is done. They made their choice and they didn't choose me. Just have to live with it. I can't fix the fact that they don't want to be my friends. I'm probably meant to be a loner."

# Answers: Let's Break It Down

a. Catastrophic; b. Mind Reading; c. Set in Stone

All these choices are chock-full of faulty logic and negative thoughts. What if we had a time machine and sent you back for a redo? What if you used some of those trusty solutions that we listed before? Try to match the action with the proper tool!

## Rewiring Tools

- Change the channel
- Write it down and rip it up
- Tell yourself the "maybe" story
- Hit the Pause button
- Look at positive images

## Actions

a. You tell your-self that maybe your friends had a sleepover because Sonya's mom didn't want to leave her daughter at home alone overnight and called Tori's mom because she knew her better than your mom. Both girls were embarrassed at the

idea that it was a bit of a babysitting-each-other situation, so they didn't say anything to you.

b. You type up all of your catastrophic thoughts and print them out, ball them up, and then turn them into toys for your dog. OK, so now there's a mess to clean up, but you got them all out of your head.

c. You start cleaning out your closet or pinning room redecoration ideas on your Pinterest board. It's much healthier to take that kind of detour.

d. You remind yourself of other things that might make you feel good by looking at some of your favorite pictures—of holidays or pets or other friends. It will help calm all the hurt feelings in your brain.

e. Before getting all that incredible exercise leaping to dramatic conclusions, you take a minute to lie on your bed and count the cracks in your ceiling.

## Answers: Let's Break It Down

a. Tell yourself the "maybe" story; b. Write it down and rip it up; c. Change the channel; d. Look at positive images; e. Hit the Pause button

Learning to take control of your brain may be one of the most powerful things you can do for your confidence, and for your life. Use your new skills as you look at part 2 of "Alex vs. Her Brain." Maybe glance back at part 1 of her story again. Notice how catastrophic thinking pulls her into a pit of anxiety, and then how focusing on something she's looking forward to gets her out.

# ALEX VS. HER BRAIN, PART 2

# GIRLS OF ACTION

Fourteen-year-old Cordelia Longo found herself facing an issue that can be super awkward for any girl: dealing with her period at school when she didn't have supplies. She attempted to buy a sanitary pad and a tampon from the dispensers in one of the bathrooms in her middle school in Seattle. But the machines ate all her change and she was left empty-handed. How embarrassing. Then she had to chase down a janitor and ask for his help. Ugh.

Some people might have just moved on afterward, but Cordelia stayed outraged. "Girls don't choose to have periods," she argued. She didn't think girls should be embarrassed by a normal bodily function because supplies aren't free or machines are broken.

Cordelia is someone who likes to keep track of women she admires, and the stories of her female heroes inspired her to do something. She's Asian American, and her ancestors, the Iu Mien, struggled hard for human rights. "That motivated me to fight for my own rights, and for other women."

She started a campaign to make these necessary

products accessible and free at school. She circulated a petition and sent appeals to the principal and school board. In her letters, she argued, "As toilet paper and tissue are used for normal bodily functions, sanitary pads and tampons are also necessary to address normal bodily functions that happen naturally. The only difference is that only girls need pads." In the meantime, she and her mom bought baskets of supplies and put them in the bathrooms, with inspirational quotes. Eventually, the school board agreed, and so the supplies are now provided for free in both her middle school and the local high school, too. She told us, "I just wanted to make people's lives better—and girls' lives easier."

# CHAPTER 6

## CONFIDENT FRIENDSHIP

### The Friendship Fall

Undertake this maneuver only in the company of true BFFs!

You know that feeling you have when you're with a good friend—the special happiness, joy, warmth, and sense of being safe that comes from knowing someone totally gets you? If you're convinced that time with your friends is as important as food or air, you're absolutely right. Scientists have discovered that friendship makes you stronger, healthier, and happier. And it turns out that friendships are pretty much the best place for testing and nurturing your confidence skills.

# FRIENDSHIP FACTS

- ◇ Friendship lowers your chance of heart disease and helps you live longer.
- ◇ When you're around your friends, you pump out oxytocin, a feel-good hormone that helps you stay calm and happy.
- ◇ One study even showed that not having strong friendships is as unhealthy as smoking.
- ◇ If you put a girl in a room and ask her do something she hates, like public speaking or touching a spider, she'll be less stressed if she's got a friend there.
- ◇ Girls who have even one good friend don't produce as much stress hormone.
- ◇ Research shows that a friend's behavior is contagious. One person's good habits tend to infect her friends—and her bad habits do, too.
- ◇ Girls' brains are wired to value their friends' approval, so caring about what other people think is normal.

# NOTICING: WHO ARE YOUR TRUE FRIENDS?

The first step in creating confidence-building friendships is figuring out who your true friends are. Does your new BFF have your back or is she really at your throat? Surrounding yourself with people who make you feel good and loved is one way to keep that confidence stockpile growing. Take a look at how Alex, Kayla, and Imani treat each other when Kayla needs support for basketball tryouts, or the way Alex's buddies pass out compliments after her lunchroom daring. That's friendship.

Here's how the girls we talked to defined friendship. A true friend:

"Is fun to hang with."

"Wants me to be happy."

"Cares about what I care about."

"Accepts me for being me."

"Is sorry when she hurts my feelings."

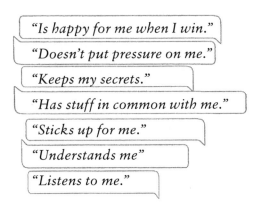

"Is happy for me when I win."

"Doesn't put pressure on me."

"Keeps my secrets."

"Has stuff in common with me."

"Sticks up for me."

"Understands me"

"Listens to me."

On the flip side, there are people who call themselves friends, but who make you feel bad in lots of different ways.

Girls gave us these tips for figuring out when someone is NOT a true friend. It's when she:

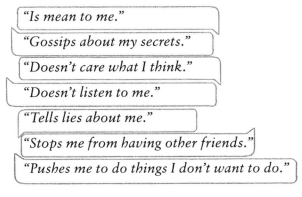

"Is mean to me."

"Gossips about my secrets."

"Doesn't care what I think."

"Doesn't listen to me."

"Tells lies about me."

"Stops me from having other friends."

"Pushes me to do things I don't want to do."

"Blames me for stuff that happens to her."

"Makes fun of me in front of other people."

"Uses me to help study, or borrows my clothes, but then disappears."

"Is competitive with me."

"Makes me feel bad about myself."

 **QUIZ**

**True Friend (TF) or Total Imposter (TI)? Try to spot the moves a real friend would make.**

1. You and your friend bought new jeans, but you think the ones she bought look pretty bad on her. She's excited about them, so you tell her she looks awesome!

2. You and your friend hang out every weekend, rain or shine. Then there's the weekend she gets invited to a sleepover and you don't. To make it worse, she won't stop talking about it, so proud that one of the popular girls included her.

3. You and your friend are debating what

to do on a Saturday. She's excited to try the new rock-climbing place. You'd rather see a movie, but you guys did that last weekend, so you smile and say, "When do we hit the boulders?"

# Answers: Let's Break It Down

1. **TF:** This is tricky, no question about it. If she's genuinely asking for your help in making a decision, then it's fine to be gently honest. But if she's really excited about them (and as her friend you can usually tell), then it's your job to be supportive!

2. **TI:** A true friend won't want to hurt your feelings, so bragging is the wrong thing to do.

3. **TF:** It's fair to take turns; you are someone who supports your friend's interests. Mutual generosity—*I give to you, you give to me*—is an important part of friendships.

What's your definition of a friend?

A true friend _____.

A total imposter _____.

In general, girls are awesome friends. (Boys are, too, but girls have all those great emotional intelligence skills to use in their relationships.) Still, we all know that friendships aren't always a piece of cake. Some friendships come easily and you practically swim along a lazy river together with no effort. Other times, it can seem scary to make a good friend, and it takes some time before you feel fully connected with that person. All friendships require effort. But making strong relationships is an essential confidence builder.

# FRIENDSHIP BASICS

Communication, communication, communication. Honest communication is the most important ingredient in confident friendships. And we don't mean texting about every move you make or every cool show you binge. We're talking about *real* communication, which sometimes means talking about stuff that makes you uncomfortable. Ever have hurt feelings? Jealousy? Anger? These kinds of emotions tend to fester and expand if you don't deal with them head-on. Opening up can feel risky, but just remember that risk-taking builds confidence.

Here are some key ways to communicate with your friends, and set the stage for powerful, healthy relationships.

**1. RECOGNIZE HOW YOU FEEL.** Peek inside your brain and take a look at what's happening. Before you can share how you feel with others, it's up to you to recognize it for yourself. The first thing

Presidential Tip on Making Unexpected Friends

President Abraham Lincoln once said, "I don't like that man. I must get to know him better." What does that mean to you? Lincoln recognized the limitations of judging people before really knowing them; he knew he might actually find something rewarding where he didn't expect it—*if* he made an effort. Are there people you're judging without knowing? Then here's a confidence challenge: think of a few kids you "don't like" and pick one to get to know. You might be surprised.

to figure out is what you're *really* feeling. Let's say that your friend didn't wait for you after school like she usually does. You might try to shrug it off and bury your feelings. Or maybe you think you feel angry. But if you examine it honestly, you're probably more *hurt*. "Why would she leave me like that? So embarrassing to stand there by myself for fifteen minutes!" Once you think you know how you *actually* feel, accept it. Don't tell yourself that it's bad to be upset. It's OK for you to have these feelings, and it's OK for your friends to have them as well.

**2. DON'T MAKE ASSUMPTIONS.** Remember all those messed-up ways of thinking we talked about? You're not a mind reader, and every bad thing is not The Worst Thing Ever. Just because two girls are whispering, don't assume they're talking about you. Just because your friend hasn't texted back doesn't mean she's mad. Also, don't assume that your friends are all-knowing. Your friend can't be blamed for not guessing that you were dying to spend the day with her. TELL her.

**3. START WITH "I."** Once you've figured out what's going on, talking it out with your friend is the healthiest option. Don't leave something simmering for a long time, or else it will boil over and make a much bigger mess! Here's the best way: start with "I." It doesn't sound like an accusation if you say "I felt hurt when . . . ," "I got upset when . . . ," or "I kind of felt like a loser when . . ." Starting with "you hurt my feelings" or "you made me feel stupid" puts your friend on the defensive and makes a fight more likely. That's not what you want to do. Instead, start with how the situation has made YOU feel. It may feel risky. You are making yourself vulnerable when you use "I." But then your friend is able to be sympathetic.

**4. OWN YOUR ROLE.** You need to take responsibility, too. Could you have done something to contribute to the problem? Think about the responsibilities of being a friend. Are you a good listener and open-hearted? Did

Ugh, what's the best thing to say to Anya?

Remember, start with me!

you start teasing her and, when she teased back, did you get upset? Own what you did and say it out loud so that you don't sound like you're blaming anyone. There is huge power in just apologizing.

5. **COME UP WITH A RESOLUTION.** It won't be perfect. It's not as neat as the solution to a math problem, because human beings don't work like equations. But figuring out a positive place to go after a problem is definitely the best next step. Usually it's a compromise. Remember, good friendships are about getting *and* giving.

 **QUIZ**

**Which sounds more like you?**

1.  For weeks, your BFF, Lindsey, has been dying to go to the opening of a cool pop-up store. It's all you guys have talked about since you first heard the news. Somehow, though, when it opens, Lindsey goes with Najayah without telling you. You figure it out on Monday morning when they're wearing new shirts and Lindsey won't meet your eye. You're super

upset. How do you respond?

a. Whatever. Fight fire with fire. Lindsey's giving you the silent treatment? You'll show her the coldest, iciest shoulder she's ever seen.

b. March over to Lindsey and Najayah and say, "Thanks for nothing! You guys went without me? You really hurt my feelings!"

c. Head to the bathroom and take some deep breaths. Splash some water on your face. Calm down. When you see Lindsey at lunch, sit down next to her like always and tell her how cute the shirt is. Then say, "Hey, that's so great that you got to go. I am a little confused, though. I thought we were going together." Let her tell you what happened.

2. You and your friend Fumi do everything together, but recently she's joined the coding club, which has started to win a whole bunch of competitions. She talks about it ALL the time. She can't hang out because she's working on new projects, or she's so busy in design sessions with her new crew. The bragging is grating on your very last nerve—how can you deal with her nonstop boasting?

a. Ignore how you're feeling—it's too embarrassing to admit. When she starts going on and on about whatever dorky thing they're doing, swallow your irritation. If you pretend nothing is wrong and nothing has changed, maybe it will just go away.

b. Clearly she's more interested in her newfound friends and her newfound fame than in being friends with you. So you start to pull away, 'cause she seems all about her new life.

c. Ask her to take a walk with you to get away from all other distractions. Think of the conversation like a sandwich: start and end with how great it is that she's rocking robotics and that you're so proud of her! Then take a risk, even though you know it could make her mad: let her know you've been feeling a little jealous and left out, which is hard for you to admit, but you also don't want to lose her friendship.

3. Your friend Sophie is boatloads of fun, except that she's obsessed with being "best friends." She buys you matching bracelets and charm necklaces and wants to do EVERYTHING

together, even plan your outfits. She gets upset when you post pictures with other friends or when you can't hang out every minute of every day, or when you change your hairstyle without consulting her. You don't want to dump her, but how can you tell her that you can't be locked down in one single friendship?

a. You can't tell her. You're trapped. Besides, it's better to have a super-good friend than no friends. There's nothing you can do about it; she'll be like a rock around your neck for the rest of your life.

b. Dodge her calls. "Forget" to answer her texts. Lie about your weekend plans. It's like playing the board game Stratego—outmaneuver her attempts to pin you down.

c. Make a plan for how to talk to her. Rehearse what you want to say so you avoid hurting her feelings. Let her know how much you want to be friends, but tell her you're not into labels like "BFFs." Use "I" statements, so that you don't sound accusatory, like "I feel all this pressure," or "I like lots of close friends, and you are definitely one of my closest friends!"

**4.** Your friend Vera confesses her enormous crush on Sam to you. All three of you walk home together every day, usually stopping to buy chips and then sharing them along the way. Now that you know about her crush, you feel this awkwardness around the two of them. One day, when Vera is home sick, you make a joke to Sam about the secret crush. It seemed funny at the time, except now Sam is weird around Vera, and Vera knows you spilled the beans. She's hurt and upset.

    **a.** OMG. You feel awful and you don't even know why you did that. It's not like you to be such a blabbermouth. Maybe you were a little jealous? Or maybe you were mad at her for changing your usual dynamic with Sam? You are completely baffled, so you just bottle up your confusion and hope the whole thing blows over.

    **b.** You can't stand how upset Vera looks, so you say, "Whatever. I did tell Sam. Who cares? It's your own fault, you should never have trusted me!"

    **c.** Take a long, hard look at yourself—is this

the kind of friend you want to be? No, probably not. So, tell Vera that you are truly sorry for what you did, with a sincere apology. Admit that you did something stupid and ask how you can make it up to her.

## Answers: Let's Break It Down

If you answered mostly **A**s, then it looks like you need to get to the heart of what's bugging you. You can't just pretend nothing's wrong. What are you really upset about? Are you hanging out in a comfort zone of denial, or staying in a bad friendship out of habit?

If you answered mostly **B**s, then you're trapped in a different kind of faulty thinking that pushes you to overreact. Catastrophize much? Are you a mind reader? Try to break it down and get out of the faulty thinking cycle, so you can take right, not rash, actions.

If you answered mostly **C**s, then you're pretty good at expressing your feelings and you approach friendships with confidence and a willingness to be open and honest. If you answered even one **C**, that's a good start to building confident friendships.

# NEW FRIENDS, CONFIDENTLY

We all know the expression "Make new friends, but keep the old. One is silver and the other gold." No matter what precious metal new friends are, it's not always easy to make them, but it is ALWAYS great to have them. The process forces you to become more confident, because approaching new people can be scary and can seem risky. In fact, way back in that risk-taking section, LOTS of girls told us that meeting new people was their biggest fear. But once you reach out, it almost always pays off and helps you create confidence. Friends don't have to be just like you. Remember to stay flexible and be open to different personalities!

Here's what some girls had to say about the art of making new friends:

> "*Don't judge. You might think,* cheerleaders are really stuck up, *or chess players are massively boring, but you could be missing out.*"

> "*If you seem gloomy, people aren't going to want to ask you to sit with them. Try to seem positive!*"

*"Think about how the other kid feels. If you just think about me me me, then it's harder to make friends."*

*"Be open to different kinds of people. Like, if you are an athlete, you can be friends with a drama kid."*

*"Always be nice to the new girl. It's way harder for her than for you!"*

*"Ask people what is their favorite WHATEVER. Anything. Book, song, dog, color. Asking questions always breaks the ice."*

*"Give a compliment! Not fake, but totally real."*

 **QUIZ**

*Madison wants to go to the movies with her new friend Cassie this weekend, but that would mean having to come right out and ask her. And who knows what might happen? Cassie might just blow her off; she might laugh at the idea of wasting precious weekend time with Madison; she might be busy with someone way cooler. All sorts of terrible outcomes zoom into Madison's brain.*

**What should Madison do?**

　　a. Mention the movie casually to Cassie at

school. "I'm dying to see that movie this weekend—I hear it's sooo good."

b. Do a bit of detective work. Talk about weekend plans in general and wait to see if Cassie already has something planned.

c. Find a moment alone with Cassie and then ask the question directly. Keep it low key, no pressure. Worst-case scenario, she says, "No way!"

# Answers: Let's Break It Down

All the options work pretty well, but some show more confidence than others.

a. If Madison goes this route, she does try, but she stays in her comfort zone and leaves room for misunderstanding. If Cassie doesn't say anything, it may just be that she didn't get the hint. Or she might actually want to see a movie with Madison, just not THAT movie. Madison might spend time overthinking simply because she didn't take a risk.

b. Not the dumbest move ever, but still not the most confident. She's avoiding risk by not putting herself out there. Again, plenty of room for overthinking and misunderstanding.

c. This is the most confident option. It'll be tough if she says no, but at least Madison will know where she stands. Now all she needs is a plan if Cassie does say no. First off, there may be a perfectly good reason, like maybe Cassie's grounded for robbing a bank. (OK, probably not that, but really, who knows with new girls? You can never tell.) If she says no, Madison can't let herself fall into a dark hole of self-pity, swearing off ever making friends again. Madison was fine before Cassie came to her school. So, she should pick up her phone and text someone else to go to the movie!

## TOXIC FRIENDS & FRENEMIES: CONFIDENCE KILLERS

Let's say you think you have a great friend. You like the same music and you like to play basketball and you both obsessively read graphic novels. Excellent start, definitely. But your friendship also yo-yos, with one minute of closeness and then ten minutes of criticism. How come it seems so hard to know when and whether she'll be mean and make you feel like dirt? It boils down to this: if she doesn't love you as you are, if she wants to change or control you, then she's probably more like a frenemy. It can be tough to spot a frenemy, and that relationship can be toxic to you and your confidence.

## CONFIDENCE CLOSE-UP

Halle has been friends with Banni since they were five years old. Now that they are twelve, Halle never knows what to expect when she sees Banni. Will it be sweet Banni who hugs her and wants to chill on beanbag chairs? Or mean Banni? Mean Banni is sarcastic and snarky and makes Halle feel terrible. She rolls her eyes about Halle's clothes or laughs about Halle's hair, constantly making little cracks.

One day Banni says something so cutting about the way Halle talks that it devastates Halle. She tries to tell Banni how she feels, but Mean Banni explodes with nastiness. Halle realizes that this is NOT a real friendship. It's too upsetting and negative all the time. She decides to talk to her mom and make a plan. She'll meet Banni in person and tell her that this whole thing's not good for either one of them.

When confronted, Banni gets furious, yelling and screaming about what a loser Halle will be without her. It's awful, yet Halle feels relief right away. She's clearly better off away from either Banni.

Ending unhealthy friendships might be scarier than seeing a tarantula—might be scarier than jumping off a mountain. It might be the scariest thing you've ever confronted, but the poison from a toxic friendship is sure to eat away at your confidence.

## BULLIES

We all know bullies—aggressive, taunting, name-calling, snickering people who seem to thrive on making other people miserable. They're less subtle than frenemies and often impossible to avoid. You need tools.

What makes a bully? Here's what girls told us.

> *"Telling lies."*

> *"Joining in the laughing at someone else."*

> *"Making people feel bad."*

> *"Faking niceness or compliments to be mean."*

> *"Picking on people who are different."*

And here are some comebacks we got from girls.

> *"I can't believe you just said that."*

> *"Hmm . . . interesting—NOT."*

> *"Leave her alone."*

> *"It's not funny unless everyone is laughing."*

> *"I don't think you meant that."*

 **QUIZ**

**There are other ways to handle a bully. Ever heard of an upstander? An upstander stands up for**

herself and for other people, instead of just being a **bystander** while someone else gets bullied.

**How would you handle these bullies?**

1. In the cafeteria, you notice a kid with Down syndrome sitting alone at a table being bullied by a group of mean girls, who are teasing him and fluffing his hair.

   a. You decide he'd be too embarrassed if you went over there and made a scene. So you sit on the other side of the room.

   b. You throw your apple core at the mean group and start to yell at them, threatening to ruffle *their* hair.

   c. You keep your cool. You walk over and ask him if you can sit down and eat with him. You say to the mean girls, "Nobody thinks you are funny. Why don't you just go away?"

2. In the bathroom at school, you watch the biggest bully in your grade barring the door to Monika, a girl who wears sporty clothes, saying, "Um, sorry, this bathroom is for REAL girls only."

   a. You stay in your stall and wait for it to blow over.

b. You shove the bully out of the way, knocking her to the ground, then say to Monika, "It's all yours!"

c. You take a deep breath to stay calm. You walk over to Monika and say, "Hi! Ignore her, she just wishes she were as cool as you are. I'll wait for you and we can walk back to class together."

3. After gym, you notice that Pilar dropped all her clothes on the floor of the shower. Now she has to put on soaking-wet clothes. Some of the popular girls are pointing and chuckling, so you can't help yelling out, "Hey, Pilar, need an umbrella?" Everyone laughs harder, but you feel awful.

a. You slink out of the locker room. What's done is done, nothing you can do about it now.

b. You run into the showers fully clothed. At least Pilar won't be the only one sitting in class dripping wet.

c. As soon you say it, you feel awful. You go right up to Pilar and tell her you're sorry. You grab extra towels from the closet and help her crouch under the hand dryer. That night, you text her to make sure she feels better and you decide to hang out with her after gym next time, so you can hold her clothes and she can hold yours. Then nobody's will get soaked.

# Answers: Let's Break It Down

If you picked **A**s, you might want to work on standing up to the bullies in your midst. Avoidance is not very effective.

If you picked **B**s, you might want hit the Pause button for a second before charging ahead. You don't want to become a bully yourself!

If you picked **C**s, then you've got incredible **upstander** instincts!

If bullying gets dangerous though, or scary, then you need to tell your parents, a teacher, a coach, or any adult. That's not the same as being a tattletale—it's the smart thing to do to stand up for yourself or your friends.

# CAN WE TALK? CONFIDENT LANGUAGE DOS AND DON'TS

"I want to tell my friends how I feel, but I'm afraid they'll be mad at me," says Louisa.

No question about it, straight talk can be hard talk. But you have to do it, with good friends and frenemies alike. How about a script with some ideas for how to translate the emotion in your head into something constructive coming out of your mouth? We got these ideas from the girls we interviewed. See if they might work for you.

If you're upset about something, bring it up when you are face-to-face. Then try something like:

*"Hey, can we talk later? I want to ask you something."*

*"Hey, do you have a second? I really need to sort something out."*

*"Remember the other day?"*

*"What do you think about . . . ?"*

*"I feel like . . ."*

*"Can you help me work this out?"*

If your friend is doing something you don't like, what about trying one of these?

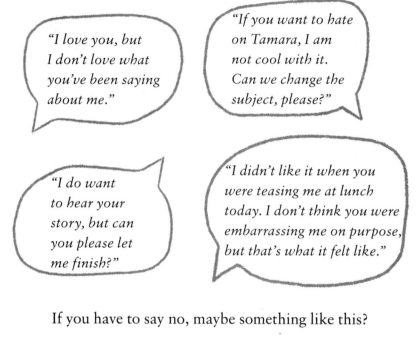

"I love you, but I don't love what you've been saying about me."

"If you want to hate on Tamara, I am not cool with it. Can we change the subject, please?"

"I do want to hear your story, but can you please let me finish?"

"I didn't like it when you were teasing me at lunch today. I don't think you were embarrassing me on purpose, but that's what it felt like."

If you have to say no, maybe something like this?

"I'm so sorry. I'd love to, but I can't figure it out today. Another time?"

"I don't like scary movies, but how about one like _____?"

"Thanks for thinking of me. But it's not my thing. You guys go ahead."

"I'm sorry . . . but I have SO much homework. UGH!"

"Sorry, darn, I can't . . . but let me know how it goes!"

Hey, can we talk? I was totally embarrassed when you were teasing me.

OMG, I'm so so sorry, and I'm so glad you told me!

Practice these, and maybe even keep a list of them nearby. Having a ready script in tough moments can really give your friendships a shot of confidence.

# GIRLS OF ACTION

Fourteen-year-old Aneeza Arshad feels like she has to be careful in every aspect of her life. Although she was born in the US, her family is Muslim and from Pakistan. Some of the women in her family wear hijabs, and recently they've endured taunting and staring due to their religion or skin color. An aunt, who's a doctor in a hospital in Texas, was knocked down by people trying to tear off her hijab. Other friends of hers have been bullied. Aneeza is sadly aware of the risks of simply walking around as a Muslim. For years she found herself trying to be two different people—a Muslim girl with her friends from the mosque, and a "typical" American girl with others from school.

When she started a new high school, those worlds collided—everyone was suddenly on the same campus. She felt nervous and awkward, finally realizing she had to just be herself and bring all her friends together. "I'm a spiritual person, so I prayed and talked to my mom, who is a trooper. My mom went through so much to be here, I like to think that if she did that, I can do the hard stuff, too."

Her friends were super supportive, and it turned out they all liked each other. With new confidence from her group of diverse buddies, she and two other Muslim friends took a big risk and started a branch of a Muslim Students' Association at school. It was a little intimidating initially, to be so public about her faith, and scary to make a proposal to their principal about their goals and hopes for their group. But they did it, and her non-Muslim friends supported her. Their MSA is starting to grow, little by little. Next year, Aneeza hopes to organize an interfaith event, so that kids can learn about all the religions at their school in a healthy, open way.

# CHAPTER 7

## A CONFIDENT GIRL'S GUIDE
## TO NAVIGATING SCREENS

WHO SAYS I SPEND *TOO MUCH* TIME STARING AT MY PHONE?

**S**ocial media. It's got the power to shake your confidence like almost nothing else. It's literally everywhere, all the time, judging, enticing, excluding, and expecting. It magnifies everything, from friendships to brain spins, from risks to belly flops, by a power of gazillion. A healthy relationship with life online is super important—because social media can either be the ultimate confidence black hole, or a confidence-enhancing new universe to explore.

# CHECK YOUR STATUS

You've been surrounded by cell phones, iPads, and computers since you were born. Some of you might already have smartphones. Others might not have access yet. What ALL of you need to be aware of, however, is what's coming for you in the virtual world.

 **QUIZ**

**Test your screen smarts. TRUE OR FALSE?**
1. 90 percent of teenagers go online every day.
2. 10 percent of teens say they feel addicted to their phones.
3. Most kids on social media say oversharing isn't a big issue.
4. Most kids think they can be more "themselves" and more "authentic" online.
5. One-third of all private pictures sent or shared become public.

# Answers: Let's Break It Down

1. True. Actually, 92 percent of teens are online every day.
2. False. 50 percent of teens feel addicted to their phones.
3. False. 88 percent think oversharing is a big issue.
4. False. 77 percent of teens think they are *less* authentic and real online.
5. True. OMG, scary, right?

When it comes to your confidence, technology can be incredible. Screens can connect you to your friends and communities of people who are a lot like you. Your phone or computer can help you find support for risk-taking, for being a Girl of Action.

But it can also be bad. And when it's bad, it's really bad. Life online tends to crank up the speed on all that brain spinning we already do so well. If you're obsessing about something that happened during class, it's tough to leave it at school and chill out at night, because you're constantly connected. You can start texting about it, posting sad pictures or advice quizzes, soliciting opinions for hours and tracking your likes. All of that only makes the obsession worse. Your brain never gets a rest.

Using devices with confidence is the goal. Use them as tools for good. Don't let them make the bad thinking get worse. Take it from an awesome young woman just a little older than you are.

## GIRL GURU

Samera Paz, who's twenty-three, is one of our Girls of Action. When she was a teenager, she remembers getting caught up in trying to please people and present a perfect image. "It was so stressful. Horrible," she remembers. She's here to offer a warning: "Things can get cloudy and murky on social media, with TONS of ways to misunderstand, to jump to conclusions. Nothing compares to sharing emotions, opinions, and vulnerabilities in person. It's so hard to distinguish between what's real and what's not online, it's easy to create a fake version of yourself, and even easier to get addicted to the likes and followers and so-called friends."

 # QUIZ

Do you have a problem? Answer these questions and be brutally honest. Keep track of your answers and prepare to do math at the end!

**Do you check your phone/device . . .**

1. Every hour (or even every few minutes)?
2. A few times a day?
3. When you need to know something specific, like the time for practice?

**Do you message your friends . . .**

1. Every hour (or even every few minutes)?
2. A few times a day?
3. When you have something specific to say?

**Do you care if you see your friends in photos online, doing things without you?**

1. Care? You might as well be dead when that happens.
2. It's the like a punch in the gut. You're wild for an hour or so, but then you catch your breath and you move on.
3. Of course, but you turn off your phone

and try to remember that it happens with everyone.

**Do you feel bad about yourself if you don't get many likes?**

1. You live for likes and followers, of course. The more the merrier!

2. You try not to check too much, but you secretly crave those likes.

3. It's fun when someone likes your Boomerang, but mostly you just want to make another one!

**Do you stress about how you look in photos?**

1. Of course. You're all about the perfect filter and lens and crop so you can look awesome.

2. You only post the best ones, even if that means sometimes you don't post at all.

3. Stress? Nah. The goofier the better—that's how you roll.

**Do you say things online that you later regret?**

1. Sure, but whatever. It's easy to get caught up in making fun of people—nobody takes it seriously.

2. Yes, but usually you're just following someone else's lead.

3. Not really. You're extra careful about what you say.

# Answers: Let's Break It Down

Add up your points by giving yourself one point for each #1, two points for each #2, and three points for each #3.

What did you get? If the total is between six and eight, you're in deep—officially obsessed. It's OK . . . it can happen to all of us. But you need to build some new roads away from this obsession.

If you scored between nine and fourteen, you're definitely addicted. Occasionally you're able to take a step back and live out your life off the screen, but keep reading this chapter for ideas on how to be even more empowered.

If you scored fifteen or higher, you're impressively balanced. You use social media when you want to and then walk away. Or maybe you just don't have much access yet. Either way, some rock-solid strategies will help keep that balance.

# WHAT NOT TO DO: CONFIDENCE-BUSTING SCREEN USE

## FULL-ON PHONE FIASCO

TEST YOUR SKILLS IN THIS
WACKY NEW GAME OF BRAIN-SPINNING
MADNESS! HELP THESE GIRLS, WHO FIND
THEMSELVES TANGLED IN TWISTED THINKING,
TERRIBLE TECHNOLOGICAL TRAVAILS, AND
SENSELESS SCREEN SILLINESS.

Remember our toolbox for combatting faulty thinking?
All those tools help for screen crises, too. And we've
added a few more.

- ⭐ Change the channel.
- ⭐ Hit the Pause button.
- ⭐ Use positive images/thinking.

☆ Find a lucky charm.

☆ Ride in a hot air balloon.

☆ Tell yourself the "maybe" story.

☆ Put the device down. Sometimes even five minutes is enough to avert a crisis.

☆ Keep it out of sight. When you can see your phone, your stress levels are higher.

☆ Take a screen vacation. Try this for more serious problems, like phone addiction.

☆ Use the 24-hour rule. Before you dash off an explosive text, give it a day.

☆ Talk face-to-face, or at least FaceTime to FaceTime, for the big stuff.


Now, mix and match from both lists to stop the brain spins.

## Dilemma #1

Tara is way into Snapchat. She sends snaps to her friends for hours at a time, including lots of people she's never met in person. She tries hard to keep the streak going and never have a break because she has big-time FOMO. Last week she freaked when she saw pictures of her friends doing stuff without her. In her mind, that meant only one thing: they obviously don't want to be friends with her at all. Her world is officially over. She figures she should send a mean message to all of them, dumping them before they can do it to her.

## Solution #1

Tara is already a **catastrophic thinker** and a bit of a **mind reader,** too, since she's sure she knows what her friends are thinking. Snapchat is only making it worse. Tara decides to put the phone aside. Then she remembers it would be useful to get another perspective. What was she doing when her friends took those pictures—maybe something important? Oh, right, she was winning a soccer game. Now she's starting to feel better!

For the BIG money: Which tools do you notice Tara using?

      a. Put the device down

      b. Tell yourself the "maybe" story

      c. Face-to-face

Um—the first two, duh! Easy right?

## Dilemma #2

Rosie's always liked to get everything right. She loves to arrange her room just so or cover her notebooks with the perfect stickers. Now that she's older, she spends loads of time on Instagram, creating the ideal image to share with the world. It's awesome, but it's exhausting: making sure to get her hair and her clothes just right, or shooting the coolest short videos. She gets lots of likes, which she LOVES, but it's stressful to always be the best, funniest, prettiest, coolest version of herself. Some days she wants to back off, but she's too afraid getting fewer likes might mean she'll becomes a total loser, and her friends might dump her.

## Solution #2

Rosie also thinks in a **catastrophic** kind of way, fearing that less posting and popularity online might mean the end of her social life. It's almost like she's wearing a mask, and her screen addiction won't let her take it off. She gets so many compliments, but do people even mean it? Rosie needs to wean herself away from the obsession, so she takes baby steps toward getting off her phone. Maybe first she moves from ten posts a day to five, and then two, then every other day, and, finally, no posts for a week. And then a complete week away from her phone if possible.

Now, let's try this again. Which of these three tools does Rosie use? What did you spot?

a. Positive thinking

b. 24-hour rule

c. Take a screen vacation

If you picked **C**, then you are ALL over this answer. She didn't, in this case, choose to put her phone down for twenty-four hours, so **B** is not correct, and she didn't employ positive thinking, so **A** isn't right either. Instead she's moving toward a solid screen vacation.

## Dilemma #3

Kiki and her friend Daria text all the time. Last night, Kiki was mad at another friend, Willow, so she went off about her to Daria over text. She was caught up in the moment, and now she barely remembers what she wrote except that it was harsh. Whew! What a relief to get that off her chest. She never meant for her ranting to go further than Daria, but Daria thought it was hilarious and forwarded it to a couple of people, and they forwarded it to a couple of people, and now everyone has seen it. Kiki never meant for this to happen. If it weren't out there, captured permanently for all to see, she might be able to fix it. But there's nothing she can do about it. Maybe she'll just stay home for a week. Or a year.

## Solution #3

Kiki believes everything is **set in stone.** No solutions in sight. She's right in one sense—there's almost NO way to guarantee privacy. Anything you type on a screen can be shared with the whole world. But, there are always ways to mend a mess. First of all, she turned to her mom, who helped her to step back and examine the problem as if she were up in the air looking down at it. From that viewpoint, she realized that the best thing is always to talk in person. She gathered her courage and went to see Willow, who was great about hashing it out. They said some tough stuff, but wound up feeling much better.

Final round. Which tools did you notice Kiki using?

    a. Ride in a hot air balloon

    b. Face-to-face

    c. 24-hour rule

Well? Yep, you got it. **A** and **B**. She pulled out plenty of tools for this one, and she figured out a way to get herself put back together!

## FUN FACT: THE CHOCOLATE ALIBI

Don't beat yourself up if you've had these kinds of phone fiascos. Most girls (and most women, too) believe that having some kind of status on social media is desirable. It turns out it's part of the wiring in our brains. Researchers have found that the same part of the brain—the ventral striatum, or pleasure center—lights up when we eat chocolate, win the lottery, OR when we get likes and views online.

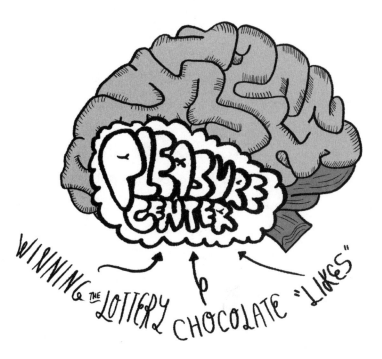

## CONFIDENCE CLOSE-UP

Robyn loves keeping in touch online with her friends from camp, her team, and school. It's fun to be able to talk to so many people at once. And even though she tries to steer clear of the drama, it's just everywhere. For every mean comment or hurtful put-down, someone says, "Just kidding!" or "Can't you take a joke?" which makes it even harder to tell what's going on. Is it bullying or teasing? She's spoken up repeatedly, telling people when she thinks they are rude or unkind. Lots of times, she becomes the bad guy, as if she's overreacting or she's the enemy of fun.

Recently, a jerk from school drew a swastika on a picture of another kid and posted it online. Robyn's family is Jewish and she felt strongly about this display. Nothing funny about it, not at all. She responded, "Hey, dude. Take it down. It's insulting." Robyn knows that racial, religious, or sexist slurs are ALWAYS inappropriate, whether people think they're joking or not. When the jerk refused to delete the picture, Robyn wanted to do more. She talked to her parents and they helped her file an official complaint with the website. Then she changed her privacy settings and blocked, unfriended, and unfollowed that kid and all the others who'd made her feel bad. After a few days, the photo was taken down. YES!

## Cyberbullying

Here's a sad truth: 95 percent of teenagers have noticed bullying online. Unfortunately, 66 percent have joined in. Nine out of ten kids witness it, but ignore it. Yikes. It's everywhere. So what are some solutions?

• Refusing to respond to nasty comments can sometimes shut a bully down.

• If you think the situation is getting worse, then tell the bully to stop. Let her know that YOU see her for what she is. A simple "that's bullying" can do the trick.

• Pay attention and keep track. Don't delete a nasty comment or photo online, even if it's tempting to want to make it go away. In fact, take screenshots. Save every example. You might need them.

• If it gets bad or threatening, find an adult (parent, teacher, coach, or counselor) to help you figure out what to do.

# WHAT TO DO: CONFIDENCE-BOOSTING SCREEN USE

There are plenty of ways to use social media for incredible good, including sharing your life with friends, collaborating on projects for school, making music, getting to understand other points of view, and connecting with people who have the same passions. Let's focus on the positives!

Here are some of the amazing ways to use the power of online communities to make the world a better place, for you and for people around you:

- ◆ Find inspiring people to follow and watch who will encourage you to do amazing things.
- ◆ Connect to people like you, positive people who will help you to be your best self.
- ◆ Use it to make a difference in your world—big or small—to be one of the Girls of Action.

We found some **Girls of Action** who've used social media in amazing ways.

◊ A middle-school girl created a Tumblr campaign to raise money to fight the kind of cancer afflicting her dad.

◊ An eleven-year-old set up an online book club to celebrate books by African American writers.

◊ A transgender high schooler launched an online campaign to promote equal rights for LGBTQ kids when she was forbidden from running for prom queen because she, as her school says, wasn't "born a girl."

◊ A group of kids in middle school started a chat group for other kids in their town who felt at risk of hurting themselves.

◊ A teenage girl ran her own news outlet to collect and share stories relevant to other kids.

◊ A twelve-year-old girl made a YouTube video to educate people about autism, because her brother is often the victim of bullies.

◊ A ten-year-old set up her own cutting-edge fashion blog, featuring clothes she and her friends designed.

Some girls we talked to shared what they love about being online.

> "Kids can support each other when they are depressed or are the targets of bullying."

> "It helps to have a bunch of different friend groups, so that you always have somewhere to turn."

> "You can find all kinds of heroes or guides!"

> "Even if you think you are the only one, you can always find people somewhere who are like you or like what you like."

## GIRL GURU

As an ambassador for Girl Power Meetups, seventeen-year-old Olivia Trice is something of a social media mastermind. She says one lesson she's learned is to use social media deliberately and consciously. "Know going into it what you want from the app—Facebook, Instagram, Twitter, or whatever it is. Define your reason for doing it, what you are hoping to accomplish. Are you trying to make new friends? Are you trying to expand awareness of whatever you care about? Are you trying to connect with people to HELP them? All the apps are very different, so you want to make sure to use them properly."

And she says it's important to remember that "not everything you see is what it is. It's not going to make your life better. It should be used to enhance you, to express you, but not to make you into a false kind of perfect. Social media encourages people to be everything else but themselves—it can encourage you to be a fake, bland version of yourself." Olivia, who's African American, points out that social media can be fraught with extra pressure for girls like her. "Black girls and girls of color need to learn to love their differences—the things that make them different from everyone. We all do. The goal for everyone is—be yourself."

Top ten strategies from girls to help navigate the world online:

"If I'm mad, I make myself wait before I send anything. Literally, I hide the phone. I eat a snack, jump in the shower, do anything I can to slow down the train in my head."

"Don't post lots of vacation pictures. Like one or two. Nobody likes it when you seem like you're bragging."

"Use all caps CAREFULLY! They can be FUN, or TOO MUCH!"

"Don't bother to lie to a friend about hanging with someone else, because it's too easy to get caught. One photo gets posted and you're toast. Just have faith in telling the truth."

"There's no way to control what people put out there about you. So just try to control what you put out there about yourself and ask your friends to do the same!"

"Forget quantity, just think about quality! Keep your circle to your true friends; then you can trust them and be yourself."

"My friends and I have parties now in high school where we check our phones at the door. We actually have a blast—even more fun than before."

"I say something out loud four times before I hit Send. It helps me to think about how I sound."

"Using more words is better. 'Sry' can look insincere or snotty. Say something like, 'I wish I could come over, but I have to walk my dogs. How about tomorrow?'"

"Think before you hit Send when it involves a picture. Would you care if your grandma saw it? Or your worst enemy? If you would, then delete it! You never know who could forward what!"

And above all, like Samera says, "Enjoy life without a phone in your hand!"

# THE GRANDMA TEST

# GIRLS OF ACTION

A few years ago, Samera Paz started to notice something. "I loved meeting other girls online or at parties and events, but then it was always hard to make a friend in that short a span of time. I wanted a sharing space, a place with no judgment where we could really get to know each other." So she started a movement called Girl Power Meetups to create space for girls her age and younger to meet on their own terms to build friendships, tackle social change, and learn how to look at the world around them with sharp, keen eyes (like you are doing with all the detecting and noticing!). As a girl of color, she was also feeling, as she puts it, "alone, young, and insignificant."

She decided to launch Girl Power Meetups on Instagram, an ideal place to reach girls, keep them interested with accessible posts and photos and inspirational quotes, expand that community, and encourage the new friendships. Where better to reach out to girls in a positive, healthy way than where they are already meeting up? But the key to GPM is monthly, in-person meetups, with themes like self-love, body image, and mental health, to encourage honest, vulnerable conversations in a sharing space with no judgments: a safe space for girls of color and all girls. "Life, school, relationships, and the future are hard enough," she explains. "I wanted a space where people could just listen and be there for one another." GPM members also take part in social activism, including projects with women's and homeless shelters and protests against police brutality.

Samera does this as a labor of love, along with her ambassadors, like Olivia Trice. She pays for Girl Power Meetups out of her own pocket, because she believes in community work and wants to empower girls who will grow up to be powerful women.

## PIECING TOGETHER THE CODE

These three chapters all boil down to another crucial piece of code: *Think Less!*

1.  Risk More!
2.  Think Less!
3.  _____

Just as *Risk More* is a quick reminder to take action, *Think Less* is a short way to prompt you to get out of your own head and obsess less. It may sound kind of funny (probably the opposite of what you think your teachers and parents want you to do!). But less brain spinning will help you confidently handle friends, social media, and almost everything else that pops up in your life.

SECTION 3

# THE CONFIDENT SELF

# IMANI FINDS HER POWER, PART 1

TO BE CONTINUED . . .

# CHAPTER 8

## KICKING THE PERFECTIONISM HABIT

### STOMP OUT THE P-WORD

**D**oes Imani's struggle in "Imani Finds Her Power" feel familiar? There's just so much to get *exactly right* in life.

Make good grades at school ✔

Keep room clean ✔

Excel at sports ✔

Be great at extracurriculars: drama, debate, math club ✔

Please parents ✔

Look good on social media ✔

Have lots of friends on social media ✔

Get invited to every cool party or event ✔

Save up spending money from babysitting, pet sitting, chores, etc. ✔

_____ (Insert your goals here.)

The list is endless.

And we really believe that, once we conquer our list, everything will be **PERFECT**.

And life will be full of:

**Blue skies and rainbows and unicorns**

or

**Pizza and beach trips and furry rugs**

or

**Trophies and big-screen TVs and awesome music**

or

---

(Insert your idea of a perfect paradise.)

And then we can finally relax. Right? RIGHT????

Wrong.

It's literally impossible to be perfect or to do everything perfectly—humans simply aren't perfect; that's not how we're made.

**If perfection is your goal, YOU'LL NEVER REACH IT.**

Like a cat chasing a shadow, you'll always be after something you can't quite catch.

**Per·fec·tion·ism:**

**Forget the dictionary definition; here's ours:**

**A really dangerous disease. An invasive, strangling vine that creeps into your life and chokes everything in its path. It stresses you out and keeps you from taking risks. And most importantly, it keeps you from being you.**

# DIAGNOSING PERFECTIONISM

The first weapon against perfectionism is simply noticing it.

 **QUIZ**

**Take a look at these girls and see whether you can recognize who's been stung by the perfectionist bug.**

a. *Tara wins the Student of the Year award in seventh grade. Super exciting, right? Not for Tara. She can't even bask in her success. All she thinks about is how her older brother won that award every year in junior high. She should have won in sixth grade, but didn't. And what if she can't win it again?*

b. *Rashida is an incredible baker. She makes elaborate cakes and pastries for family celebrations, getting heaps of praise for her beautiful creations. Still, she obsesses about the tiny mistakes she makes in the fancy icing flowers and swirls. When her uncle asks her to design his wedding cake, she's scared to take the chance in case she messes it up.*

c. *Andrea wants to work out more, so she draws up an ambitious schedule to run every morning before school and do laps at the local pool every afternoon. She does it perfectly for a week, and then life gets in the way. One morning, she wakes up too late and doesn't run. The next, she's got an orthodontist appointment*

## Girls and Perfectionism: A Super-Short Flowchart

**From a very young age, your girl-brain strengths give you advantages.**

You listen better, do what you're told, try hard—all that stuff. ↓

Adults like that behavior (it's easier for them!) and reward it. ↓

You like being rewarded (who doesn't?) and so work even harder at everything.

↓

Perfectionists and people-pleasers are born.

**What about boys?**

They mess up a lot because they can't help it.

But . . . ↓

They learn that failure and risk are OK. ↓

And they get confident.

The end. (Until we change the story.)

*after school so she can't make it to the pool. Andrea realizes she's been unrealistic and needs to make a more workable plan. Three days a week is good enough.*

d. *Maura has had weeks to work on her social studies diorama, but kept putting it off. It needs to be perfect—her creations always impress everyone. The night before it's due, she leaps into action, racing around, building, gluing, printing out captions. She spills glue all over the project, but manages to scrape most of it off. In the end, she's exhausted and she's made some silly mistakes, but she's got to turn it in!*

# Answers: Let's Break It Down

If you picked **A**, **B**, and **D**, you nailed it. These are all different faces of perfectionism. In **A**, not being able to celebrate accomplishments is classic perfectionism. In **B**, perfectionism stops Rashida from taking a risk, even though she wants to do it. And in **D**, Maura shows us another aspect of perfectionist behavior— procrastination. Maura undermines herself by waiting for the perfect time, which never comes. In **C**, however, Andrea shows flexibility. She starts out with a perfectionistic, rigid goal, but she's able to dial it back to something more reasonable.

## QUIZ

**Are you addicted to the quest for perfection? Jot down a yes or no for each scenario below and we'll look at it together at the end.**

- You've just cleaned up your room, but that new pillow isn't working, the posters on the wall look ridiculous, and you can't get anything else done. When things aren't "right," it *really* bugs you.
- You get a high score (a 92!) on your science test. After one moment of elation, you look around and spy a 98 on Lena's test. Suddenly, you feel like a loser.
- You check your Insta likes. Up by twenty! But other people still have way more. You'd better think about improving your camera angles and content.

✯ You get a part in the musical, plus a solo. But you can't feel good about it because, well, other people have bigger parts.

✯ You have *lots* of ideas about things you want to try. But you're afraid to take the risks unless you can do them well. So nothing happens.

✯ There's a constant message playing in your head, going over little mistakes you've made—stupid things you said, things you wish you'd done, blah, blah, blah.

✯ You feel like an imposter, like you've fooled everyone, when you do well.

✯ If you can't sit in just the right place at lunch, with just the right people, your day is basically ruined.

✯ You want to make conversation with a new kid, but feel boring and predictable. You'll avoid him until you can come up with the funniest, coolest things to say.

✯ You compare yourself to other girls 24/7, which leaves you feeling awful.

Take a look at your notebook. How many times did you say yes?

## Answers: Let's Break It Down

1–4: Not bad! You like to do some things well, but aren't infected with the perfection disease. Pat yourself on the back.

5–7: Hmm . . . Some hints of "I must be perfect" here. Of course, you want to be good at things, but watch out for the slippery slope of *having* to be good at *everything*. Work on a sense of balance before it's too late.

8–10: DANGER, DANGER! Perfectionism alert! Do you ever just chill? Time to take five of those *yes* answers and toss them in the trash. Being good-enough-but-not-perfect won't hurt you, or kill you. In fact, it will make you stronger.

## WHAT'S THE BIG DEAL?

A lot of girls we talked with didn't understand why perfectionism is such a problem.

Here are some common perfectionism misconceptions.

> "Isn't perfectionism kind of good, though? I mean, isn't that really the way to succeed?"

> "Doesn't it just mean I'm ambitious?"

> "Being perfect is a good way to make people happy, isn't it?"

> "Trying to be perfect means I'm working hard and pushing myself, right?"

## NONE OF THOSE THINGS ARE TRUE.

Perfectionism isn't the key to success, or anything else in life. Perfectionism is basically all those faulty thinking patterns we talked about before, rolled into one—like a giant burrito of flawed ideas.

Think about it:

♦ It's literally an impossible standard.

♦ Trying to be perfect is exhausting and no fun.

♦ You're working for the wrong reasons.

(Perfectionism usually goes hand in hand with

**people-pleasing**, another dangerous disease.)

✦ And most importantly, if you're a perfectionist, **you can't build confidence.**

Here's why:

When your goal is to do everything perfectly, you

really

really

really

really really really really really really really really

really really

really really really really

**don't want to fail.**

The idea of failure

**freaks you out.**

If you aren't willing to fail, as we've already learned, you won't want to take risks or action. And then you won't be building confidence. Look again at part 1 of "Imani Finds Her Power." Trying to be the best is overwhelming Imani, literally shutting her down.

# GIRL GURU

Lori Lindsey has done some pretty amazing things in her life. A professional women's soccer player, she was on the

US Women's National Team and the Olympic team in 2012, and she's played in the World Cup. She wants you to know that perfectionism gave her nothing but trouble. "I wish I'd had more strategies when I was younger to just chill out. I overanalyzed and overthought—I was so busy being a perfectionist, trying to make it all happen on the field, and that often stole the joy and flow of playing from me. And I didn't play my best. When I could let go of the perfectionism and just play, I was able to let the game come to me. Whatever you're doing, ask yourself why. And what you're really trying to get out of it. Then the magic happens."

## PERFECTIONISM CURES

**DO IT FOR PURPOSE, NOT PERFECTION OR APPROVAL.**
Ask yourself some questions like, "Who am I doing this for?" or "Why am I doing this?" Girls and women can get trapped by the disease to please—trying to make everyone happy but ourselves. (Thank you, high EQ.) If you find yourself thinking excessively about what others want or constantly telling yourself you "should" do things, that's a warning bell. Think about

your goals and make sure they come from inside, not elsewhere.

**CHANGE THE FINISH LINE.** What's the goal? If the goal is ONLY to be perfect or achieve perfection, swap it out. If you're working toward a finish line (winning a tournament, getting an A, having the most followers, etc.), look at that finish line again. Is it realistic? Is it something you really want? If not, try setting some reasonable goals.

**GOOD ENOUGH.** It works. Do the best with what you've got and give yourself permission NOT to do the most perfect, most accomplished, most amazing job of all time. Time is precious. Do what you can and move on. Good is *absolutely* good enough, and you'll find out later in life that it's often a better approach. Want proof now? Here's some great data. Grown women typically won't apply for a job or a promotion unless they think they are perfectly prepared and have all the necessary skills. Guys apply even if they only have 60 percent of the skills. Guess what—the less-qualified men get the jobs because they decided they're good enough and just go for it. SO—here's a real challenge: Pick one assignment, give yourself a time limit, do the best you can IN THAT TIME, and declare it "good enough."

**TALK TO YOUR PARENTS.** Lots of times, adults make things even worse, with pressure about grades, activities, and appearance. It's hard even for them to resist the stranglehold of perfectionism. Be honest with them. If they have unrealistic expectations and are stressing you out, they should know.

**REMAKE YOUR CHECKLIST.** Remember that checklist from the beginning of the chapter? Rethink that—it doesn't need to handcuff you to the idea of perfection. List the coolest stuff you do or want to do. Celebrate all the things you've tried, even if you failed at them. If perfectionism shuts all the doors and windows that lead to uncertainty, the possibility of adventure, and even failure—then force them open!

GOOD ENOUGH     VS.     PERFECT

**FOCUS ON NOW.** Perfectionism is about living in the past or the future. Have you noticed that you spend a lot of time thinking about what went wrong, or what you need to get done? Get your mind focused on today—this instant. That's where you find confidence and joy.

## PERFECTIONISM-BUSTING LANGUAGE

Next time a perfectionistic thought is buzzing around your head, or you hear yourself uttering a perfectionistic phrase, try to swap it out.

Whenever you think, "**I should**," always ask yourself, "Why?"

When you think, "**It has to be perfect**," replace it with "That's good enough!"

If you think, "**I'm not very good at that**," replace it with "I will give it a TRY!"

If you say, "**I've gotta win**," or "**I've gotta be first**," replace it with "I want to enjoy the ride and have fun along the way."

## CONFIDENCE CLOSE-UP

Eleven-year-old Faith gets anxious about homework, feeling like something is pressing down on her. She puts it off and puts it off, making it worse. In her mind, she thinks that if she waits, there will be a perfect time to do it, a perfect time when she's not hungry or grumpy or sick of hearing her little brother shouting. THEN she will do the best job possible ... as long as it's later. She has a project for the fifth-grade science fair at school: make a clock with a potato as the battery. She's really scared her project will look lame next to all the others. Their poster boards will be more incredible than hers, their projects better looking. She doesn't want to be embarrassed, so she just keeps putting it off. Surely, the perfect solution will occur to her.

Finally, the deadline's staring Faith in the face. She knows she needs to get on with it, so she calms herself down by repeating, "It's not a big deal." She talks it over with her mom and realizes that she's actually excited to see if she can make the potato work as a battery so who cares about the finished project? It doesn't have to be the best of the best, it just has to be good enough. In the end, it's not perfect, not amazing, but totally good. And that's how she feels, too!

# MIRROR, MIRROR

Perfectionism may be at its most dangerous, and at its most toxic to confidence, when we apply it to how we think we should look. If you worry about your appearance—and feel like you're failing—there's good reason. Everywhere you look, you see gorgeous people with perfect bodies and perfect hair and perfect teeth and perfect clothes. Looking great can seem like one more thing to add to your list. It can feel almost impossible to fight the pressure. And for girls of color, it might feel like you have to represent your entire race or culture. If you aren't perfect, then that will reflect badly on anyone else who looks like you.

The pressure on girls is massive. If you're feeling it, we have a few helpful weapons for you.

# WEAPON 1: KNOW YOU ARE NOT ALONE!

- ✮ 92 percent of teen girls would like to change something about the way they look.
- ✮ Nine out of ten girls feel pressure by fashion and media industries to be skinny.
- ✮ 53 percent of American girls are unhappy with their bodies by the time they are thirteen. By seventeen, that goes up to 78 percent.
- ✮ Eight in ten girls opt out of sports, school activities, getting together with friends—the fun stuff of life, in other words!—if they don't feel good about how they look.
- ✮ Seven in ten girls don't want to assert themselves or stand up for their opinions if they aren't happy with how they look.

# WEAPON 2: TAKE A GOOD LOOK!

It's time to be a culture critic once again. Media and our culture are the reason so many girls and women worry about how they look. Not only are you not alone, you are not to blame. Most of the glamorous images you see on websites or in magazines don't represent real girls and women around the world. They can make us feel bad about ourselves because they are FAKE, and they are everywhere. Celebrities, models, and even regular people posting online require time, effort, and money (for celebrities, an enormous team of specialists!) to show the best angles possible. And then they are photoshopped to hide any and all imperfections.

Girls like you are becoming aware, and that helps bring change:

★ Seven out ten girls think the media puts too much pressure on them to achieve a narrow standard of beauty.

And many girls and women are starting to demand change. Check out the Stop the Photoshop campaign online.

## YOUR TURN

One way to combat those images for yourself is to whip out your Confidence Notebook or phone or piece of paper once again and check out your role models. Now, think of them through the lens of how they look:

◊ Do they seem airbrushed and posed?

- ◊ Do they seem active and powerful?
- ◊ Find people who are willing to be themselves, who are DOING something (playing, running, making, writing, creating, trying to make a difference).
- ◊ Find people who match the way you are feeling, the way you want to live.
- ◊ Search for strong people looking natural: no makeup, unstraightened hair, clothes that allow them to do, not just to pose.
- ◊ Don't limit your role models to famous people, take a good look at people you see every day.

## WEAPON 3: TREAT YOURSELF THE WAY YOU TREAT OTHERS!

Eighty-two percent of girls believe every woman has something about her that is beautiful. So learn to see yourself the way others no doubt see you. **KEEP IN MIND:** Since there's NO perfect way to look, all combinations and variations are powerful. All of them.

## WEAPON 4: DON'T JUST BE. DO!

Obsessing about what you look like, or paying too much attention to your appearance, is static not active. And it's a waste of time. Plain and simple. Think about it for a minute. It doesn't add to the world or your accomplishments or challenges. It stops you from jumping into stuff you want to do and it takes your attention away from everything that's going on in your life. Which means, that's right, you aren't building confidence. Who you are and what you do matter way more than how you look.

Always remember: Confident girls value action over appearance.

# GIRLS OF ACTION

When Gloria Lucas was ten years old, she didn't like herself or her body. Her mother and father moved to California from Mexico, and Gloria had the idea, like a lot of girls of color, that she didn't fit an "American" ideal. "My mom once came home with the brown Barbie doll. I made her return it, because I wanted the white one." Gloria started struggling with eating disorders and had a hard time finding help. "I never saw somebody who looked like me or talked like me discussing eating disorders. It wasn't talked about in our community."

She finally managed to recover from the eating disorders on her own, after years of suffering. Once out of high school, she had a sudden realization: she wanted to be that voice, that salvation, that she had never found. So she started an organization to help young girls of color understand more about healthy body image, and to give them role models, teach them resilience, and create a community. As she says, "I want to help girls figure out that when you can connect to your culture, your roots, you get power. That's very healing. It was for me, and it can be for others."

Gloria turned her painful, personal struggle into fuel to make a difference. She believes that "the work is not about me. It's something I was meant to do. It's bigger than I am." And, as she says, "DNA predetermines how we look. We can't really change it. This vessel, your body, is a gift whatever color and size. We must honor that. We belong to ourselves."

# CHAPTER 9
## BEING TRUE TO YOU

eing 100 percent, fully, truly, utterly yourself is a big part of confidence. But who are you, anyway? Sometimes, the answer to that might seem obvious. At other moments, the real you might feel like a puzzle with a lot of missing pieces.

### CONFIDENCE WARM-UP

Do you really like sports—or are you only playing because your friends play, or because your parents want you to play, or because you always have?

Are you actually passionate about being in the coding club, or are you just trying to please your favorite math teacher?

Do you lose track of time when you write poetry—but barely ever do it because, well, what does it really accomplish after all?

Do you want to make other people happy, or check things off a list, instead of doing what you like?

If you aren't entirely sure why, deep down, you choose to do or not do certain things, that's not surprising. These years can be confusing. Don't worry. They are supposed to be full of dramatic moods, frustrations with parents, and intense exploration. This is exactly the age when you start to sort it all out, experiment with who you are, and learn to tune in to yourself.

**When you listen to yourself above everybody else, you can hear your confidence, your inner voice, your confident self.**

## CONFIDENCE CLOSE-UP

Selene's starting at a new school, so she's eager to meet the right people and be popular. Her parents come from India, so she looks a little different from other kids, which makes it harder to fit in. She chooses the group of girls who have the most followers and most friends online. Having all that online attention makes these kids powerful. They expect other kids to trade them for the best lockers and the best tables at lunch. Obviously, everyone thinks they rock.

When people talk about Selene, they'll start to lump her in with this cool crowd, which will cement her reputation. The only problem is that she actually finds these girls a little boring. They don't do much except stare at their phones and take selfies. But who is she to argue with all that popularity?

Selene thought she'd found a way to take a shortcut to making friends. Instead, she took the absolute wrong path, the path that led her away from being herself. She starts signing up for the stuff she's truly interested in on the sly because her popular friends roll their eyes when she talks about her passions. The kids in the math club are pretty hilarious. Who knew that doing hard calculations as a team and then shouting out the answers could make her laugh so hard? And the drama club is awesome.

Selene's so much happier hanging out with these other kids who like what she likes, who care about what she cares about, that she starts to forget to meet up with the popular crowd. One day at lunch, she sits with other members of the drama club. After that, the popular kids stop talking to her, stop including her on their messages or inviting her to hang. Honestly, she hardly even notices. She's started to tap into her Confident Self.

Selene managed to find her path—but it's not always that easy. There are expectations coming at you from all directions, from everyone and everywhere: parents, teachers, and friends on the one hand; images on TV, magazines, movies, YouTube, and social media on the other. And for anyone who feels "different"—as many tweens and teens do at some point—there can be extra layers of pressure about who you should be.

It's exhausting trying to be someone else, to act or speak or dress or move or look or sound like someone else. It never works very well, and it sucks your confidence dry.

**"Be yourself, everyone else is already taken."**

Nobody really knows who uttered this brilliant bit of wisdom first, but we love it.

## FINDING YOU

When you're trying to get a clear picture of who you are, it helps to start with these dependable lenses.

**VALUES.** Values are like your guiding lights, your beliefs, the ideas that matter most to you and help you decide how to act. Sometimes you're not even aware of your values until you focus on them. If you uncover that you care intensely about generosity, for example, then the kind of thing you've always done naturally might start to make sense: you will even more readily devote time to helping your friends, sharing with your siblings, or volunteering, because you will see it's who you are.

There are so many different values that we can't put them all here, but take a look at this short list to see if anything motivates you. Do these ring a bell?

Honesty

Compassion

Gratitude

Family

Determination

Wisdom

Love

Courage

Creativity

Optimism

**TRUE STRENGTHS.** Another way to nail down who you are is to think about your true strengths. An ability is a true strength when it meets three requirements.

◊ You're pretty good at it or have some kind of skill.

◊ You're passionate about it. (Nobody has to nag you to do it.)

◊ It brings you joy. (When you are practicing the activity or skill, you often lose track of time and get lost in the "flow.")

There's an endless list of possible true strengths, of course. To figure out yours, think about them in different ways: they can be specific things you've learned to do well, like math or spelling or knitting or dribbling a ball. Or they can be broader abilities that come a little more naturally to you, like being funny or being curious or having a great sense of direction or maybe being fast.

But don't forget the passion and joy! (The flow thing is really cool when you feel it. It's when you just totally lose track of everything else because your brain and interests and passion are all in sync. One scientist calls it the definition of happiness.)

Here's a real-life example. Casey is a total math genius—it comes easily to her—but math is not her favorite thing. She doesn't much care about the problem solving. She's much more passionate about people and their stories, and she's a terrific listener, totally losing herself in their tales. Being able to connect with people and being sympathetic are definite strengths for her.

Of course, there are way, way, way too many to include all of them, but here's a short list of some strengths. If you want to dive deeper, we've listed some great resources in the back of the book.

Working with numbers

Using humor

Playing sports

Being fast
Being a good listener
Being a great reader
Being artistic
connecting with others
Being sympathetic
Being a leader
Being musical

## YOUR TURN

To figure out your strengths, think about:

    What makes you feel good while you are doing it?

    What gives you energy?

    What do you do that makes you happy?

    What do you do a lot, on your own, without
        ever being reminded?

    What kind of things do you notice in the world?

    What kind of things make you excited?

    What kind of things cause you to lose track
        of time? (Social media quicksand doesn't
        count!)

**THE VALUES/STRENGTHS CONNECTION.** When you find *overlap* between your strengths and your values, it's like a warp-speed boost. Confidence flows much more naturally. Take Casey. One of her values is family, and she's especially close to her grandparents, who used to live at home with her. Now that they're in a nursing home, Casey really enjoys hanging out there, playing games and reading with the old folks. Her true strengths of sympathy and connecting PLUS her value of family are acting together to let her be her truest self.

### CONFIDENCE WARM-UP

Pull out your Confidence Notebook and draw a line down the center of a page. Put your answers to the **Strengths** questions on one side and pick out five of your most important **Values** to write on the other. Now take a look. Do you see a pattern? Do you see connections?

Here's a sample from Billie's Confidence Notebook.

## STRENGTHS Q'S

What makes you feel good while you are doing it?

**Knitting**

What gives you energy?

**Spending time by myself to recharge**

What do you do that makes you happy?

**Solving word puzzles**

What do you do a lot, on your own, without ever being reminded?

**Reading about politics and current events, so that I feel like I understand what's going on better**

What kind of things do you notice when you pay attention to the outside world?

**The way certain people are treated better than others**

What kind of things make you excited?

**Figuring out solutions to problems**

What kind of things cause you to lose track of time?

Knitting, reading, watching news programs

## MY VALUES
Wisdom
Compassion
Creativity
Courage
Optimism

When Billie looks over her two lists, she sees some connections. She values wisdom—and is passionate about politics and problem solving. No wonder the debate team has always seemed intriguing! And now that she sees creativity on the page, as one of her values, her passion for knitting makes sense. She decides she doesn't have to feel guilty about that time she spends alone with her needles and yarn.

Start thinking about what's important to you, what you love, and what you enjoy doing. You may jot down only a few things now—but don't worry, the list will grow and change. Of course, there are some things young people are just stuck with, like school and chores and other family work. But there's still plenty of YOU time. And if you start to discover how to be true to yourself now, you are much more likely to spend your life doing what matters to you, instead of what everyone else wants you to do or thinks is good for you.

## CONFIDENCE CLOSE-UP

Poppy had always thought of herself as not very interested in athletic stuff. She'd tried soccer and volleyball but had never really taken to team sports. Then, when she was eleven, she found herself transfixed by the dancers in the school musical. Just watching those girls leap across the stage made her happy. She begged her mom to find her dance classes, but when she learned all the girls her age at the local ballet school had been taking classes since they were little, she almost dropped the whole plan. She was really intimidated. It's a stupid idea, she told herself— there was no way she would ever keep up, and she'd look like such a baby.

Poppy hated the idea of missing out on the feeling of being able to bend so gracefully or spin so smoothly. In her mind she could see herself doing it. Still, being a beginner in a class full of experts terrified her. Eventually her mom persuaded her to try just one class. If she hated it, she could quit. That way it seemed more low-key, just a casual tryout, which helped her. No big deal. In the end she needn't have worried. The teacher made her so welcome, the other girls helped her with the complicated ballet positions, and she managed to follow along just fine.

Was she perfect? Of course not. Was she as good as the others? No way, how could she be? They'd done it for years. But Poppy realized she was good enough, and more importantly, she had so much fun she stopped focusing on how she compared and just let herself enjoy dancing. She'd clearly tapped into a natural passion.

## CONFIDENCE CONUNDRUM:
### Untangling What Makes You You

How can these girls realize their strengths and their values and focus on them, so they can be true to themselves?

1. *Hailey's schedule is packed. She plays tennis and piano. When she's on the court, she loses track*

*of time. She only hears the sound of the ball being thwacked and only sees the distinctive neon-green orb flying through the air. She's constantly strategizing about alternate shots, or other ways to approach the net for a smash volley. Practicing piano is a bit of a bore, but she loves playing keyboard in her band and has fun with the other kids, writing songs and performing. She gets to be creative in both tennis and band, which helps her feel confident and optimistic.*

*Hailey keeps winning tennis matches, which means that she misses band rehearsals and piano lessons. She doesn't make it to a couple big shows with her band because she can't get back from a match in time. No matter what, it seems like someone is always mad at her: her bandmates for blowing them off or her piano teacher for coming in late or her coach when her parents whisk her away as soon as she steps off the court. And there's always homework, which she winds up doing in the car or late at night. Now, she's fried. She needs to figure out how to be true to herself, so that she's not running around in circles.*

<blockquote>
a. Looks like Hailey's overwhelmed. Her teachers always tell her that school comes first. Maybe she should just stop doing all
</blockquote>

these extracurriculars and take things easy.

b. Tennis is her favorite, hands down. Hailey needs to ditch the piano, even if she likes playing in the band.

c. Hailey needs to be honest with her parents and explain how she's feeling. Tennis makes her the happiest, but that doesn't mean she wants to throw everything else away. Tennis is totally joyful, but music harnesses her creativity. Maybe she can stop taking lessons but stay in the band, with more flexible rehearsals, tapping into both of her creative outlets.

2. *Emma is obsessed with animals. She volunteers for any and all dog-, cat-, fish-, gerbil-, bunny- or even lizard-sitting jobs she can find because being around creatures makes her feel calm, strong, and powerful. She loves taking care of them, even when it involves digging a scoop into a bucket of wriggling crickets to feed the lizards. She signed up for an after-school life science class. Sure, sometimes the class is a bit dull, but it's helping her be more of an expert on the creatures she loves, so she's determined to do it.*

*It turns out that her friends are annoyed with her. They all used to go over to each other's houses, gulp down snacks, and listen to music. Now, they're grumpy that she doesn't seem as into THEM as she is into this whole animal thing. Emma tries explaining how good it makes her feel to have a skittish kitten trust her, to help a scared dog learn to sniff the outside world, or to know the right way to feed a bizarre lizard. But they just keep saying that she's a weirdo for liking animals more than she likes them. Are they right? How can Emma reconcile her interests and her friends and still be true to herself?*

a. If Emma wants to keep her friends, she should drop the class and scale back on all the animal duties. Hanging with her BFFs is the normal thing to do. Plus, she doesn't want to have a reputation as a weirdo.

b. She should drop the after-school class, definitely. If she speeds up all the animal care after school, rushing to get it done, then she can race to still get to hang out with her friends.

c. She needs to try talking to her friends sincerely, heart-to-heart. Maybe they'd think it was fun to help with some of the animals? It is her obvious passion. If they still call her "weirdo," then are they true friends? Maybe hanging out with more understanding kids would allow Emma to be more herself.

# Answers: Let's Break It Down

All these stories have clues about what makes these girls uniquely themselves. Did you catch them?

In the **A** answers, each girl lets other people define who she is or what she should do. The soundtracks of teachers, friends, and parents are playing in their heads. Hailey and Emma decide to just quit doing the things that make them their truest selves.

In the **B** answers, each girl tries halfway solutions. These may not be the worst situations, but the girls still don't get to be their most authentic selves. Hailey keeps tennis but loses her connection to her band. Emma works on getting her friends to understand her animal passion, but gives up the science class (she values wisdom, so that's a defeat).

In the **C** answers, both girls take the strongest stand to be totally themselves. It all starts with being honest

## Born That Way?

Are people really born with natural strengths, or amazing talent? Sometimes it seems like it. You know the type. They're so great at *everything*—athletic stars, honor students, class presidents—plus it all seems so easy for them.

Well—not necessarily.

It's true that we all come with *some* natural skills. Certain kids have exceptional reflexes or amazing hand-eye coordination, or there are kids who can memorize vocabulary at the speed of light, or kids whose doodles are better than the art teacher's. So, yeah, maybe they started life with some abilities, but that's just the beginning.

Scientists have discovered that the real powers behind those gold medalists, award-winning performers, and trailblazing thinkers are **grit and a growth mindset.** Grit is a willingness to fail and

and open and understanding their values and strengths. Asking her parents for help, Hailey strives to make room for both tennis and music. Emma realizes that true friends should let her be herself, animal obsession and all.

## CONFIDENCE CLOSE-UP

Everyone always thinks of Madelyn as the quiet, dreamy bookworm. Everyone except Madelyn herself. She's always noticing the way girls are treated compared to boys. The subtle and not-so-subtle stereotyping. After thinking about it for a long time, she pipes up to her parents that she wants to go to an all-girls school, where the environment can be totally about girls and their accomplishments.

Once she starts the new school, all her new friends are on sports teams: girls' volleyball in the fall, girls' basketball through the winter, and girls' softball in the spring. That's a problem. Madelyn can't run or catch or do anything remotely worthy of being on a team, and she doesn't want to sit in the bleachers and read. She wants to be in the thick of it, like her athletic friends. Her mom suggests cheerleading, but Madelyn says, "No way!" She pictures cheerleaders on the sidelines, flouncing around and clapping for boys.

"But . . . wait a minute," she thinks, "maybe I need to open up my mind. I'd be cheering keep going again and again, and a growth mindset is a belief that you can always learn and improve. Some researchers say grit is more important than brains when it comes to success. And a growth mindset really helps, because intelligence and skills and excellence *can* be learned. When you operate with those two things, you achieve.

So, ask any of the talented girls and women out there— including people like Serena Williams or Laurie Hernandez or Beyoncé—what it takes. Or read about women like astrophysicist Sara Seager, who's helped to discover hundreds of new planets and is obsessed with finding the next Earth. They will all say it's the work and repetition and attitude that make the difference. It only looks like a natural strength to us, watching from the outside.

for girls—my friends!" She believes in powerful girls, and she would love to jump up and down and scream from the top of her lungs about it. But she's held back because of, um, a stereotype of a cheerleader? She came to this school to stop being defined by other people's ideas about what she or other girls should be. Why not be her OWN version of a cheerleader for all those GIRLS doing powerful amazing things?

Madelyn makes the squad and surprises her whole family. A cheerleader, not a bookworm? Stomping, yelling, and leading the cheers for strong girl athletes—now Madelyn has opened up her mind and is doing what she believes in. Being her own true self.

# MIRROR, MIRROR REVISITED

There's no way to stress this enough, except to keep saying it: BE YOURSELF. And that means LOOK LIKE YOURSELF, too.

For some girls, looking authentic equals gym shorts and a comfy T-shirt. For others, it means vintage sweaters and a twirly skirt or cutting-edge creations sewn by hand. It's all terrific. There's no right or wrong style. If you use your clothes to express yourself, then you are the only one who has to like them. (Well, parents kind of need to be on board, too.)

Having your outside (your appearance) match your inside (your sense of self) is easy to take for granted. For some kids, like Toni in our next close-up, their bodies may not match their true selves, and then they have to take the brave step of revealing themselves to the world, especially when that self is unexpected or unconventional. These kinds of kids battle to literally *be* themselves, so looking like their true selves and dressing like their true selves is an incredible victory.

## CONFIDENCE CLOSE-UP

For as long as she can remember, Toni has felt that she was in the wrong body. When she was born, her birth certificate said "male." For the first few years of her life, everyone called her a boy. The first time she started to show her friends her real self was during a second-grade "share." Even though she was still "Tony," in boys' sweatpants and a T-shirt, she brought in lipstick to share with the class. She was lucky, because her friends in her class, the girls and the boys, were curious, and mostly cool and supportive. So Toni started to show, in small ways, the person she was at her core. She started wearing more "girl" things, like a barrette, a headband, and then nail polish and bracelets. She changed the spelling of her name from Tony to Toni, writing TONI in big loopy letters on her papers, her folders, and her lunchbox. She traded her boxy boys' T-shirts for ones with flowers and unicorns. Being a girl means different things to different girls, but for Toni, it meant the freedom to look like one. Her parents helped her go slowly, take it one step at a time. And she did. All of the adults worried that she'd be bullied, or that it was a phase, or that she'd get hurt. But Toni knew she was really just becoming the self she was always meant to be.

After months of gradually transitioning out of her boy clothes, she stepped into her first dress. Once she put it on, it perfectly reflected the person she'd always been, deep inside. There were a few kids on the playground or in the lunchroom who heckled her and made fun of her. But the kids from her second-grade class, the kids who watched her shed the old clothes and put on the right ones, those kids clustered around her, yelling back, "What are you looking at? She's just a girl!" She didn't feel alone in the wrong body anymore, she felt like her Confident Self, supported by a great community. She still doesn't think that she's done anything particularly brave or courageous; she just thinks she's finally herself.

Hear yourself. Know yourself. Understand yourself. And you'll start to feel ready for action.

# GIRLS OF ACTION

Twelve-year-old Lexi Proctor has always loved curls . . . and she has plenty of them. But in kindergarten, she was bullied by girls who said she had "bushy tree" hair and made fun of her dark skin. "I didn't understand why they'd treat me like that and I got scared to go to school. I got really self-conscious. So I changed my hair." For years, she used so much heat to straighten it that her once-lovely hair became damaged.

Then she was inspired by a picture of a dark-skinned girl with natural curly hair. "I thought, 'She is not afraid, *she* is totally confident in herself.'" The image of this brave girl grabbed Lexi and flipped a switch in her brain. She had found an incredible role model. And she knew it was time to unleash her curls. She was terrified, though, that the name-calling might start up again. But she took a long look in the mirror and told herself, "I want to be ME. I want people to see me and not a girl who is hiding who she really is. If they don't like it, too bad! It's my business. Who are they to mind my business?" She told herself that over and over, keeping in mind how relieved she'd feel to stop hiding her real self.

Once she did it, she says, "I loved it so much that I decided I wanted to write a book for kids like me. I really want to make girls feel good about themselves, especially for those girls who don't love their hair or their skin color." (Her movement is called Curlanistas!) Her first book is *Curly Girls Love Your Curls*, and her second is *The Ice Cream Talk: Loving the Skin You're In*. "The people in my family are varied colors. One time someone didn't think my grandmother *was* my grandmother, and it really hurt my feelings. My grandmother told me that people are like ice cream; they come in many flavors, but underneath they're all the same."

# CHAPTER 10

## BECOMING A GIRL OF ACTION

A ction and confidence are inseparable. You know
that by now.

Action builds confidence. Confidence helps us take action.

And all shapes and sizes of action are great. But you're now ready to start thinking about actions that aren't just for you alone. You can start thinking bigger than yourself. We call that leap moving from

ME to WE.

Here's why it's so powerful:

ⵝⵝⵝⵝ

## A TALE OF TWO ACTIONS

Close your eyes. Think about some actions that require risk, but that are more about you—like raising your hand in class, getting help from a teacher, or asking the bus driver to stop. How does that make you feel?

Now, think about taking action to help someone else. Something you would do for other people or a cause you care about, like comforting your sister when she's upset, or helping victims of a natural disaster, or trying to save endangered animals. Close your eyes again. Create a clear picture in your mind of what you would want to do. How does that make you feel?

Is there a difference between these two scenarios?

You might feel more empowered, more excited,

## Girl Boy Gurus

The brothers who cofounded the WE organization are so cool, we decided to include them, despite the fact they aren't girls! Craig and Marc Kielburger are known as *social* entrepreneurs, meaning they've started a powerful enterprise that isn't about making money. The main purpose of WE is to offer people simple tools to help create positive social change, in local communities and around the world. One of their secrets: taking passionate young people of all ages and helping them get involved. The WE team creates groups in schools, guides families looking to get involved, and coaches individual kids who come up with their own projects

When Craig was twelve, he was extremely shy, with a speech impediment. He saw an article about a boy his age in Pakistan more of a tug at your heartstrings, and a bunch of warm, fuzzy happiness when you're thinking about jumping in and helping on behalf of something outside of yourself—whether it's family, friends, clean water supply, global warming, laboratory testing on animals, poverty, or any other passion. *Me to We* is a powerful way of thinking.

## THE SCIENCE OF *ME TO WE*

Psychologists have found that switching your circuits from *me thinking* to *we thinking* does a lot of great things for your brain. Getting your mind off yourself and making others a priority will lower your stress and anxiety and give you a happiness boost. It also increases your confidence. Why? Researchers have found it gets you over the hurdle of being too self-conscious about taking a risk or taking action. Studies found that young women—recent college grads—who were nervous about new jobs were more confident when they focused less on themselves and more on how they could help their supervisors, the team, or cause.

In fact, other studies show that girls and women may be particularly drawn to the idea of helping. It might be our brains, with their

who was shot protesting child labor. Craig became haunted by the boy's death, so he summoned the courage to ask his classmates—stammering—if they would help him turn children's rights into their cause. Eleven of them said yes. That, eventually, grew into WE, which has 3.8 million young people and their families engaged around the world today. Here's his message: "You are not an adult in waiting! You don't have to wait until you are grown, or have a job with a fancy title, to get things done. If you want to change the world, start now." As you search for ideas and support, WE can be a good resource. Check them out. Keep in mind, girls are often more motivated by causes than boys. Craig told us that 80 percent (80 percent!) of his youth volunteers are girls.

more active emotional connections—scientists aren't sure. But when choosing a career, women, more than men, value a strong mission or cause, or prefer to work for a company that does something good for society. And studies show that girls will take much greater risks and actions when they are involved in a passion project.

## *ME TO WE* IN ACTION

*Leni loves the idea of running to raise money for illnesses afflicting people in her family, like epilepsy and diabetes. But her asthma makes it hard for her to sign up for a run. Her mom suggested that she volunteer to hand out water and orange slices to the runners during a local race instead. It's so great: she gets to help and feel like she's part of the solution.*

*Kennedy's favorite place in the whole world is her local library. For as long as she can remember, she's gone there almost every day: to check out a book or look around or listen in on one of the readings. So it made perfect sense for her to sign up to work at the library's book fair—organizing the books, just doing whatever she can. She had no idea how good it would feel helping people find fun things to read.*

*Chloe lives in an apartment building with no elevator. Her neighbor Carol is in her seventies and lives on the top floor with her cats. Chloe loves to listen to her funny stories and play with her cats. Carol has to haul heavy groceries, kitty litter, and laundry up five flights of stairs. Chloe worries about Carol, so she comes up with a plan for her to leave her bulky stuff on the first floor and send Chloe a text. Every time she helps bring the bags upstairs, Chloe feels a little rush.*

## WARNING: *ME* to *WE* MAKES YOUR HEART EXPAND

## ME TO WE NEEDS A STRONG YOU.

A confident girl moves into the world from a place of strength. Life will often present you with difficult, messy, and seemingly unfair challenges. Before you can advocate for others, this is another reminder that you must be your own best champion.

## A CONFIDENT GIRL'S MANIFESTO

(Read this aloud at least once a week.)

♦ I have the right to be treated with respect.

♦ I have the right to boundaries and personal space.

♦ I will speak up or take action when someone or something is making me uncomfortable.

♦ I don't always please people—that's not my job.

♦ I am loyal to friends and family, but also to my values, to doing the right thing.

♦ I am strong enough to deal with the consequences of actions I take.

♦ I will find a trusted adult when I need help.

## CONFIDENCE WARM-UP

So, now, how do you get started? Look at your lists of strengths and values. What excites you, or makes you mad? Here are some opportunities from everyday life:

1.  People at school are muttering mean things about someone, or using nasty stereotypes. You could:

    a.  Band together with friends who understand what it's like to be a target.

    b.  Talk to other supportive kids, teachers, or your guidance counselor about ways to create safe, welcoming school environments.

    c.  Get some ideas online for how to start a club to promote an antihate agenda.

2.  Mounds of garbage are stacked up outside the lunchroom because kids are too lazy to use the garbage cans. You could:

    a.  Help start a recycling and composting program.

    b.  Organize a group of kids to clean it up with you for community service hours.

c. Take pictures of it and write a story for your school newspaper.

3. The dress code really drives you nuts and makes steam come out your ears. You could:

   a. Run for student council so you can take a match (or pen) to that dress code once you're in office.

   b. Form a committee with other kids and have a meeting with the principal about how to make changes.

   c. Get together with other kids on social media and see what's worked in other schools.

Remember: you've got a lot to offer. Even when you're doing something you love, or something that doesn't seem that hard—like singing in a chorus, running for student government, or helping out an annoying sibling—there's also a benefit to other people who get to enjoy your songs, learn from your good ideas, and feel your support.

# GET INTO YOUR GROOVE: TIPS FOR BIG ACTION

When action gets really big, when it has a deeper purpose, it's called ACTIVISM.

Before you strap on your superhero cape and start trying to leap a tall building in a single bound, keep these tips in mind.

**GOAL TIME.** We've told you that science shows declaring or writing down a goal increases the chances you'll really, actually DO IT, no matter what it is. Plus, the pleasure center of your brain (remember our brain diagram?) responds to the satisfaction of setting a goal and then checking it off. Even little mini goals (eating a good breakfast or writing in your journal every day) make that pleasure center light up. But remember— don't get perfectionistic! It's really important to be FLEXIBLE with your goals. Otherwise you might miss a cool opportunity that comes your way, because it's not on your list. Adjust as you go. A goal is just a tool to help you move forward.

**DON'T GO IT ALONE!** Find people who care as much as you do about whatever you want to do. More minds get more done. Plus, it's twice as fun and inspiring.

Start talking to people, or post a petition to see who's interested. Or brainstorm with an adult you like.

*Jazmin is a bit of a loner. She feels like she's hovering on the fringes of life. She spends lots of time by herself online, obsessing about how girls around the world are denied basic education. Dwelling on this stuff can be overwhelming and can make her feel more isolated. Even though it's hard for her to put herself out there, she decides to talk to her guidance counselor about starting a girls' leadership committee to increase awareness of the problem. She and the counselor host a meeting, and lots of other girls show up. Turns out, they care as much as she does. And she really likes working and talking with them. Now they're all exploring together, and getting something done seems possible!*

**SAY IT LIKE YOU MEAN IT!** Your voice is the most powerful tool you have. The language you use helps you become a Girl of Action. Whether you are speaking in a class or writing a letter, be active, positive, and clear. And here's a great trick—remember *Me to We* when you feel nervous. You'll feel more confident if you tell yourself you are speaking for others, or about something more than just yourself. Remember, even speaking up at all, about anything, will inspire others.

*Alice noticed something that really bothered her on a school trip. The girls were all standing at the back of the pack, and none of them were raising their hands to ask questions—only the boys were. When she got home, she told her mom about it, saying she feels like girls are often just afraid to be heard—what if they make a mistake? She and her mom brought up girls and hand raising at Alice's next Girl Scout meeting. Alice and the troop decided to lobby for a new patch called the "Raise Your Hand" patch. That patch is now available for the scouts to earn—in fact, it's already sold out. The message: Girls have the information and the brains. They should have the confidence to step up, learn to lead by raising their hands. It's no big deal if you don't know the answer.*

## CONFIDENCE WARM-UP

Start to notice how you say things. Are you putting yourself down or making fun of yourself to seem more modest? We all have this habit. But avoid it when you are being a Girl of Action. YOU are powerful, so your words need to match. Check out the difference.

| What NOT to Say | What to Say |
|---|---|
| • "This may be a stupid question . . ." | • "Hello, is this a good time to talk?" |
| • "Excuse me, sorry, I hate to bother you. . . ." | • "I have a question." |
| • "I don't care, whatever . . ." | • "I'd like to see that movie, what about you?" |
| • "Um, is this project OK? I'm not sure." | • "I think this is a great project." |

**APOLOGIZING AVALANCHE.** Unnecessary apologizing is such an epidemic we decided to give it a separate category. Have you noticed that girls and women say "I'm sorry" all the time? Saying "sorry" is appropriate and kind when you've done something wrong, hurt someone's feelings, interrupted a conversation, or kept a friend waiting.

But girls often pepper communication with *sorry*s even when we've got nothing to be sorry about! Some social scientists think it's partly because we are so sensitive to other people's feelings. Some of us may think it sounds polite to tell the waiter, "Sorry, I ordered the chocolate milkshake, not the strawberry." Or that it will sound less aggressive to stick a *sorry* before "I disagree." Whatever the causes or reasons, constantly apologizing makes you sound less than confident. Check out Pantene's empowering "Not Sorry" commercial, showing women rethinking the word.

NOTICE how often you deploy the *sorry* word and think about whether you mean it. Do you start conversations with "I'm sorry" even when you're not actually sorry about anything? Are you quick to apologize for normal, everyday stuff that everyone does, like missing a shot or coming in on the wrong note or brushing by someone in the hall? Saying you're sorry only when it's really necessary will make you more direct, more powerful, and make your apologies more genuine when you actually need them.

**FEEL FREE TO BE IRRITATING!** Not everyone will welcome activism. Change isn't easy, and lots of people would rather not hear about it.

*You hate the idea that classroom pets are left alone on the weekend, in the dark, echo-filled school. You propose a sign-up sheet to your teacher for kids to take the gerbils home from Friday through Sunday. That's just one more thing for him to have to arrange, so he's a little discouraging. You decide it's worth it to be annoying, as long as you are courteous, to make those animals more comfortable. You offer to make the sign-up sheets and make sure it all goes smoothly.*

**KEEP IN MIND:** Confidence is contagious. It spreads like butter on toast when shared with friends. If you're around others who are confident and positive, your brain's prefrontal cortex—the main hub for rational thought—lights up, making you feel confident too. Studies also show that women and girls are more willing to DO risky things, to take big action, when just one friend or person they respect gives them a push. SO . . .

### CONFIDENCE WARM-UP

Tell your friend to:

> (Pull out your phone and do it now if you can!)
> Run for student council,
> Or sell her jewelry at a craft fair,
> Or try out for a team,

Or put her short stories into a book.

Or _____ (You fill it in.)

Your word has a huge impact on people. And if your friends are doers too, imagine how many people you can inspire.

You get it by now. Taking action means that you can make a difference in your world, in ways that you can define—big or small, global or personal. Take a look at part 2 of "Imani Finds Her Power." Imani's able to build confidence, eliminate some stress, and embrace "good enough" when she jumps into action on an issue she really cares about.

Find your passion and use it in a way that feels true and authentic to you and join the army of Girls of Action.

Catching Confidence!

# IMANI FINDS HER POWER, PART 2

# GIRLS OF ACTION

When Sarah Shamai was fifteen years old, her mom came back from a trip to Haiti and told her about the situation in orphanages there, including the shortage of normal things like underwear for many of the orphaned girls. "I thought about how I could not live without underwear and how it might not occur to people to donate something like that. And it is embarrassing for those girls, not to have panties or bras, and it might be too hard for them to ask somebody. I just really could understand feeling like that, and I wanted to help." But she's also shy, and overcoming that wasn't easy. She started with friends and family. "It was scary to step outside my comfort zone, but the idea of helping these girls made me feel better."

She took the first donations of underwear to Haiti with her mom, and then she was more motivated than ever. After that, she was able to make herself speak in front of groups to try to raise money. She set up a charity and a website called Haiti Undergarments for Girls (HUGs) and got to go back to Haiti several more times. "I thought it would be really small, so I was really happy and surprised that we've been able to reach this many people." Now she is expanding, selling baked goods that she and her friends make at farmers' markets in her area and getting people to sponsor her on her 5K runs. She says, "Anybody can get out there and help others; even little things add up."

## PIECING TOGETHER THE CODE

OK, so here's what should be seared into your memory from these last three chapters: *Be Yourself!*

1. Risk More!
2. Think Less!
3. Be Yourself!

This is the last piece to the code, the final golden strand. Use it to help you turn *off* perfectionistic instincts, people-pleasing tendencies, and unrealistic expectations, and to turn *on* your authentic self. There's nothing more powerful, more confident, than being you!

# CHAPTER 11

## CREATING YOUR OWN CONFIDENCE CODE

The time has come. We've covered a lot of concepts and you've worked your way through them all. You're ready to assemble your own Confidence Code.

We've given you a preview of the basic pieces at the end of each section, but we really think it might help to SEE the process of code making. Think of the next few pages as a big whiteboard. We've sketched out the way everything you've read in the book is distilled into three elements, and then how those come together into a simple but powerful Confidence Code.

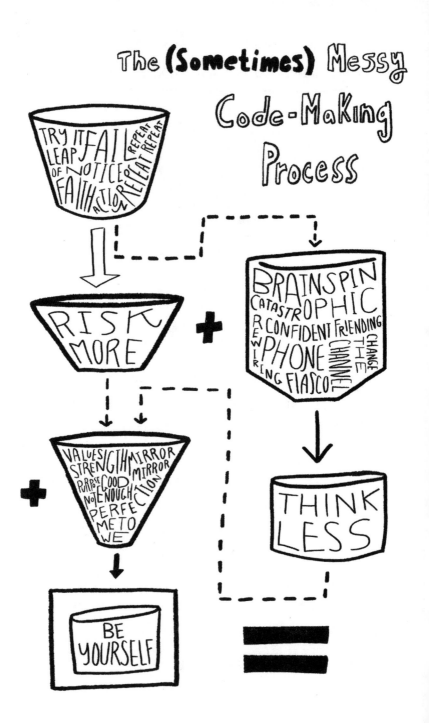

RISK MORE
+
THINK LESS
+
BE YOURSELF

The

Confidence Code

So that's how the Confidence Code is made. Here's how we like to picture the finished product:

# CUSTOMIZE YOUR CODE

Follow that code, and you are on your way to a confident life. But not every code needs to say *Risk More/Think Less/Be Yourself*—those are just the broad descriptions of how to build confidence. You can choose what suits you. Like looking at a menu, pick whatever seems appealing! (We're even going to show you how to design your own code from our template online.)

Your code should be true to you by identifying how you want to tackle risks, curb your overthinking, and celebrate the real you. And once you make it, it's not set in stone. You can change it as often as you like.

To get you started, here are some sample pieces of code from other girls. You can borrow directly from any of these or simply let them inspire you.

## RISK MORE

Try something new every day

Don't hide from what seems impossible

Be brave

Never say never

Hard is awesome

Never give up

Talk to new people

## THINK LESS

Don't obsess

More fun, fewer fights

Less chat time

Take a walk

Shoot some hoops

Play some music

Tell my brain to shut up when it's spinning

## BE YOURSELF

Do stuff that matters to me

Wear what makes me happy

Be glad that I get totally lost in my book

I'm an amazing artist

Say what I really think

Be OK if people don't get me

Accept me for me

### YOUR TURN

If you're still pondering what your personal versions of *Risk More/Think Less/Be Yourself* might be, try these ways to spark your imagination. Whip out that

Confidence Notebook and take a look at the strengths and values that you wrote down from chapter 9. Does that help you define your Confidence Code? Or, take a look at the list of healthy, positive goals you made from chapter 10. Does that help you pin anything down?

Or, try thinking about it this way:

I will _____.

I won't _____.

I am _____.

Let's see what other girls have dreamed up for their codes. For Susannah, her variation on *Risk More/Think Less/Be Yourself* is:

Never back down/Stop putting things off/Dare to look different from my friends.

For India, it's:

Sit with different kids at lunch/Don't hide how I feel/Hang out with my family.

For Charlotte, it's:

Try out for one new thing every semester/Stop caring (and crying) about how many likes I get/Be as dorky as I want as long as I'm happy!

Here's Della's:

Never give up/Ignore judgment/Accept me for me

And here's Poppy's:

I will try something new every day/I won't go on my phone as much/I'll do what matters to me (ballet!)

## CODE IN ACTION

Once you're ready to put together the pieces of your code, you can either photocopy the blank one pictured on page 268, or head over to www.confidencecodegirls. com. Fill in your code and print it out to put over your desk, next to your bed, under your pillow, or anyplace else you will see it constantly. Or you can share it, pin it, or post it on social media. Totally up to you.

And you can make as many codes as you want—changing, revising, and remaking them over and over. Do it once a week, once a month, or once a year. As we said, the code is meant to reflect what makes you YOU, so it can morph all the time. Day to day, week to week, it might look completely different, and that's OK. Once your confidence starts growing, your Confidence Code will need to adapt.

Keep it front and center all the time, on your walls, in your feeds, on your mind. You'll see how following the code will become as instinctive as a muscle memory, as natural as riding a bike, reading a book, or texting on your phone.

So put this book down and go make your own Confidence Code, and let your confident life begin.

# ACKNOWLEDGMENTS

As we've worked on this project, we've benefited enormously from meaningful and unsparing help and support.

First, we want to thank our daughters, Della, Poppy, and Maya. They were our inspiration, of course, but also our fiercest champions, toughest critics, and most insightful editors.

We are eternally grateful to our coauthor and collaborator, JillEllyn Riley, who helped us get deep into the minds of girls and brought incredible passion and wisdom and organization to the project.

JillEllyn thanks Claire and Katty for including her on this confidence-building adventure—it was an honor to work alongside these strong, brilliant, powerful women, not to mention all kinds of fun.

The three of us want to give special thanks to Nan Lawson, whose captivating illustrations and graphic panels bring the book to life. We knew the final product had to be visual, full of stories, and she made *The Confidence Code for Girls* a thing of joy.

Many thanks as well to our wise and patient editor,

Sara Sargent, who has supported our vision from the start; to our incredible agent, Christy Fletcher, who astutely understands all things, including the move from women to girls; to Sylvie Greenberg, who helped make it happen with seemingly effortless grace; and to the top-notch team at HarperCollins, savvy and dedicated to creating something distinctive and unique for girls: Suzanne Murphy, Kate Jackson, Andrea Pappenheimer, Barbara Fitzsimmons, Alison Donalty, Michelle Cunningham, Camille Kellogg, Bethany Reis, Alana Whitman, Nellie Kurtzman, Stephanie Boyar, and Cindy Hamilton. In particular, we feel so lucky to have worked with Alison Klapthor, our design wizard, who was so patient and endlessly creative.

For all of her hard work and determination and resourcefulness on everything from fact checking to uncovering **Girls of Action**, we thank our dogged researcher, Hannah Lapham Tucker.

This book couldn't have happened without the dozens and dozens (and dozens!) of girls we talked to from all across the country. We thank them and their parents for trusting us with their stories and experiences, their vulnerabilities and triumphs, their confidence nightmares and their confident aspirations. Throughout the book, we've changed many of their names to protect their privacy. Their voices infuse the book with relevance and meaning and humor.

In particular, we appreciate the following girls for sharing so much of their time: Alana, Alexandra, Angelica, Anu, Ashley, Avery, Bella, Bianca, Carine, Celia, Edyth, Eva, Grace, Janvi, Juliette (Jules), Malia, Mary Beth, Mia, Mikala, Morgan, Nora, Penelope, Rosaylin, Ruby, Sofia, Soleil, Sophie, Vrunda, and Willa.

We are indebted to our **Girls of Action** for stepping forward and being heard: Aneeza Arshad, Shiloh Gonsky, Gracie Kuglin, Olivia Lee, Cordelia Longo, Gloria Lucas, Samera Paz, Lexi Proctor, Sarah Shamai, and Amaiya Zafar.

And a big thanks to our young editors/readers group: Ava Gregory, Asmi Pareek, Liane Bolduc, Sasha and Romy Ugel, Emma Gutnikoff, Antonia Brooks, and Mia Green. Their thoughtful edits made the book so much better.

Although this project comes out of the work and research for our adult book, *The Confidence Code for Girls* is in fact an entirely different animal. We were determined to make it engaging and interactive, packed with CBT techniques that could truly help change habits and mindsets. We wanted the quizzes, scenarios, and tips to be grounded in science and delivered in ways that would speak to girls. And for that, we needed guidance, so we are grateful to have had the help of three special gurus: Rachel Simmons, Bonnie Zucker, and

Phyllis Fagell—all of them were willing to read and advise and tell us candidly what would and would not work. They gave us an enormous confidence boost.

For more inspiration and support, we are tremendously appreciative of Susannah Shakow, Wanda Holland Green, Sherica White, Caroline Miller, Weezie Parry, Desha Golden, Marissa Rauch, Craig Kielburger, and Jim Steyer.

Heaps of gratitude to Ariel Aberg-Riger, Heather Myers, and the whole Spark No. 9 team for their generous gift of time and creativity on the project.

Katty thanks her sons, Felix and Jude, for being kind and loving, and Tom for keeping his frazzled wife calm and providing his sons and daughters with such a great role model. And Awa for her friendship, wisdom, and endless smiles.

Claire is grateful to her son, Hugo, who offered encouragement, baseball tips at critical moments, and so many hugs; Jay, who yet again helped her believe a new path was possible; and Janet, who kept her laughing and juggled the circus simultaneously.

JillEllyn is eternally grateful to Caroline, Jessica, Jodi, Kathryn, Kim, Lori, Matthew, Melissa, Meredith, Nely, Patricia, and Penina for sage advice and generous counsel. To Alan, Cullen, and Eoin—big heart, big love. For Miles, as always.

# RESOURCES

There are so many incredible writers, scholars, researchers, and social scientists doing tremendous work with and for girls, and it's a thrill to have been helped and inspired by them.

Here are some additional resources you might like, including valuable books for parents, cool ways to assess strengths and values, and great organizations for girls to check out.

# PUBLICATIONS

Alvord, Mary Karapetian, Judy Johnson Grados, and
     Bonnie Zucker. *Resilience Builder Program for Children
     and Adolescents: Enhancing Social Competence and
     Self Regulation: A Cognitive-Behavioral Approach.*
     Champaign, IL: Research Press, 2011.

Brown, Lyn Mikel. *Powered By Girl: A Field Guide for Supporting Youth Activists*. Boston: Beacon, 2016.

Cain, Susan. *Quiet Power: The Secret Strength of Introverts*. New York: Penguin, 2016.

Dweck, Carol S. *Mindset: Changing the Way You Think to Fulfil Your Potential*. London: Little, Brown, 2012.

Paul, Caroline. *The Gutsy Girl: Escapades for Your Life of Epic Adventure*. New York: Bloomsbury USA, 2017.

Radin, Stacey, and Leslie Goldman. *Brave Girls: Raising Young Women with Passion and Purpose to Become Powerful Leaders*. New York: Atria, 2016.

Rendall, David J., and Eric Smoldt. *The Freak Factor for Kids*. Raleigh, NC: SEADS, 2012.

Simmons, Rachel. *The Curse of the Good Girl: Raising Authentic Girls with Courage and Confidence*. New York: Penguin, 2010.

Waters, Lea. *The Strength Switch: How the New Science of Strength-Based Parenting Can Help Your Child and Your Teen to Flourish*. New York: Avery, 2017.

Zucker, Bonnie. *Anxiety-Free Kids: An Interactive Guide for Parents and Children*. Waco, TX: Prufrock, 2008.

# ORGANIZATIONS

For girls and their parents who are passionate about pursuing a healthy self-image, confidence, and leadership, here's a list of incredible organizations:

Amy Poehler's Smart Girls: https://amysmartgirls.com

Common Sense Media: commonsensemedia.org

Girls Inc.: https://girlsinc.org

Girls on the Run: www.girlsontherun.org

Girl Scouts of America: www.girlscouts.org

Girls Who Code: https://girlswhocode.com

Girls Write Now: www.girlswritenow.org

I Am That Girl: www.iamthatgirl.com

Running Start: https://runningstartonline.org

VIA Institute for Character: www.viacharacter.org

WE Institute: www.creatingwe.com

## ENDNOTES

### Section 1: The Keys to Confidence

### Chapter 1: The Nuts & Bolts of Confidence
**Thoughts + Confidence = Action**

We clarified this formula with the help of Dr. Richard Petty, Ohio State University; Nansook Park, University of Michigan; David Dunning, Cornell University; Joyce Ehrlinger, Washington State University; and Adam Kepecs, Cold Spring Harbor Laboratory.

Bandura, Albert. "Self-efficacy: Toward a unifying theory of behavioral change." *Psychological Review* 84, no. 2 (1977): 191–215. https://doi.org/10.1037/0033-295x .84.2.191. `

Kepecs, Adam, Naoshige Uchida, Hatim A. Zariwala, and Zachary F. Mainen. "Neural Correlates, Computation

and Behavioural Impact of Decision Confidence."
*Nature* 455, no. 7210 (2008): 227–31. https://doi.
org/10.1038/nature07200.

Park, Nansook, and Christopher Peterson. "Achieving and
Sustaining a Good Life." *Perspectives on Psychological
Science* 4 (2009): 422–28. https://doi.org/10.1111/j.1745-
6924.2009.01149.x.

Park, Nansook, and Christopher Peterson. "Positive
Psychology and Character Strengths: Application to
Strengths-Based School Counseling." *Professional
School Counseling* 12, no. 2 (2008): 85–92. https://doi.
org/10.5330/psc.n.2010-12.85.

Rosenberg, Morris. *Conceiving the Self*. New York: Basic
Books, 1979.

Seligman, Martin E. *Learned Optimism: How to Change
Your Mind and Your Life*. New York: Random House
Digital, 2011.

**Scientists have found that writing things down**

Markman, Art. "How Writing To-Do Lists Helps Your
Brain (Whether or Not You Finish Them)." *Fast
Company*, September 6, 2016. www.fastcompany.
com/3063392/how-writing-to-do-lists-helps-your-
brain-even-when-you-dont-comple.

Mueller, Pam A., and Daniel M. Oppenheimer. "The Pen Is Mightier Than the Keyboard." *Psychological Science* 25, no. 6 (2014): 1159–68. https://doi.org/10.1177/0956797614524581.

Wax, Dustin. "Writing and Remembering: Why We Remember What We Write." Lifehack. June 30, 2017. www.lifehack.org/articles/featured/writing-and-remembering-why-we-remember-what-we-write.html.

**Power Positions**

Although there has been some question about whether power positions actually change body chemistry, scientists confirm they do still lead to a *feeling* of greater power and therefore confidence:

Briñol, Pablo, Richard E. Petty, and Benjamin Wagner. "Body Posture Effects on Self-Evaluation: A Self-Validation Approach." *European Journal of Social Psychology* 39, no. 6 (2009): 1053–64. https://doi.org/10.1002/ejsp.607.

Cuddy, Amy J. C. "Want to Lean In? Try a Power Pose." *Harvard Business Review*, March 20, 2013. Accessed September 13, 2017. https://hbr.org/2013/03/want-to-lean-in-try-a-power-po-2.

**Chapter 2: Risky Business!**

**Step 5. Small Steps**

Locke, E. A., and G. P. Latham. "Building a Practically
Useful Theory of Goal Setting and Task Motivation:
A 35-Year Odyssey." *American Psychologist* 57, no. 9
(2002): 705–17. www.farmerhealth.org.au/wp-content/
uploads/2016/12/Building-a-Practically-Useful-Theory-
of-Goal-Setting-and-Task-Motivation-A-35-Year-
Odyssey.pdf.

**Step 7. Be Your Own Coach, visualize**

Adams, A. J. "Seeing Is Believing: The Power of
Visualization." *Flourish!*, December 3, 2009.
www.psychologytoday.com/blog/flourish/200912/
seeing-is-believing-the-power-visualization.

Sheard, Michael, and Jim Golby. "Effect of a Psychological
Skills Training Program on Swimming Performance
and Positive Psychological Development." *International
Journal of Sport and Exercise Psychology* 4, no.
2 (2006): 149–69. https://doi.org/10.1080/16121
97x.2006.9671790.

**Chapter 3: Epic Fail**

Well, there's actual science that shows failure creates success.

Duckworth, Angela. *Grit: The Power of Passion and Perseverance*. London: Vermilion, 2017.

Miller, Caroline Adams. *Getting Grit: The Evidence-Based Approach to Cultivating Passion, Perseverance, and Purpose*. Boulder, CO: Sounds True, 2017

Seligman, Martin E. *Learned Optimism: How to Change Your Mind and Your Life*. New York: Random House Digital, 2011.

**It is impossible to live without failing at something.**

Rowling, J. K. "The Fringe Benefits of Failure, and the Importance of Imagination." *Harvard Gazette*, June 5, 2008. https://news.harvard.edu/gazette/story/2008/06/text-of-j-k-rowling-speech.

**The reality is, sometimes you lose.**

Nessif, Bruna. "Watch: Beyoncé's Video Message Part 2." E! Online. December 17, 2013. www.eonline.com/news/491914/beyonce-says-message-behind-latest-album-is-finding-the-beauty-in-imperfection-watch-now.

**I'm not afraid of storms, for I'm learning how to sail my ship.**

Alcott, Louisa May. *Little Women*. New York: Bantam, 1886.

## 1. Be Your Own BFF

Salzberg, Sharon. *The Kindness Handbook: A Practical Companion*. Boulder, CO: Sounds True, 2008.

Salzberg, Sharon. *Real Happiness: The Power of Meditation: A 28-Day Program*. New York: Workman, 2011.

## 4. Ask for Help

"Growth Mindset Asking for Help." Teaching Superkids. October 23, 2016. www.teachingsuperkids.com/ growth-mindset-asking-for-help/.

Brown, Brené. *Daring Greatly: How the Courage to Be Vulnerable Transforms the Way We Live, Love, Parent, and Lead*. New York: Avery, 2015.

Brown, Brené. *The Gifts of Imperfection: Let Go of Who You Think You're Supposed to Be and Embrace Who You Are*. Center City, MN: Hazelden, 2010.

Brown, Brené. *Rising Strong: How the Ability to Reset Transforms the Way We Live, Love, Parent, and Lead*. New York: Random House, 2017.

Dweck, Carol S. *Mindset: Changing the Way You Think to Fulfil Your Potential*. London: Little, Brown, 2012.

Krakovsky, Marina. "Researchers: If You Want a Favor, Ask and Ask Again." *Insights*. September

19, 2013. www.gsb.stanford.edu/insights/
researchers-if-you-want-favor-ask-ask-again.

## Chapter 4: Become a Culture Critic
### Girls do better than boys in school

Voyer, Daniel, and Susan D. Voyer. "Gender Differences
in Scholastic Achievement: A Meta-analysis."
*Psychological Bulletin* 140, no. 4 (2014): 1174–204.
https://doi.org/10.1037/a0036620.

### Countries with more gender equity

Revinga, Ana, and Sudhir Shetty. "Empowering Women Is
Smart Economics." *Finance & Development*, March
2012. www.imf.org/external/pubs/ft/fandd/2012/03/
revenga.htm.

### Businesses with more female leaders

Noland, Marcus, Tyler Moran, and Barbara Kotschwar. "Is
Gender Diversity Profitable? Evidence from a Global
Survey." Peterson Institute for International Economics.
February 2016. https://piie.com/publications/wp/
wp16-3.pdf.

**Female members of Congress**

Volden, Craig, and Alan E. Wiseman. *Legislative Effectiveness in the United States Congress: The Lawmakers*. New York: Cambridge University Press, 2014.

**As of October 2017, only eleven heads of states**

"Facts and Figures: Leadership and Political Participation." UN Women. Last modified July 2017. www.unwomen.org/en/what-we-do/leadership-and-political-participation/facts-and-figures.

**Only 25 percent of jobs in science, technology, engineering, and math**

"Women in Science, Technology, Engineering, and Mathematics (STEM)." Catalyst. March 29, 2017. www.catalyst.org/knowledge/women-science-technology-engineering-and-mathematics-stem.

**Women earn about 83 percent of what men earn**

Brown, Anna, and Eileen Patten. "The Narrowing, but Persistent, Gender Gap in Pay." Pew Research Center. April 3, 2017. www.pewresearch.org/fact-tank/2017/04/03/gender-pay-gap-facts.

**In the entire US Congress (the House of Representatives and the Senate)**

"Women in the U.S. Congress 2017." CAWP. Accessed November 13, 2017. www.cawp.rutgers.edu/women-us-congress-2017.

## Section 2: Confidence Inside & Out

### Chapter 5: You & Your Brain
**Girls and women can overthink things**

Lynd-Stevenson, Robert M., and Christie M. Hearne. "Perfectionism and Depressive Affect: The Pros and Cons of Being a Perfectionist." *Personality and Individual Differences* 26, no. 3 (1999): 549–62. https://doi.org/10.1016/s0191-8869(98)00170-6.

Mitchelson, Jacqueline K. "Perfectionism." *Journal of Occupational and Organizational Psychology* 82, no. 2 (2009): 349–67. https://doi.org/10.1348/096317908x314874.

Nolen-Hoeksema, Susan, Blair E. Wisco, and Sonja Lyubomirksy. "Rethinking Rumination." *Perspectives on Psychological Science* 3, no. 5 (September 2008): 400–24. https://doi.org/10.1111/j.1745-6924.2008.00088.x.

**Check out the most common flawed thinking patterns**

Beck, Judith S. *Cognitive Behavior Therapy: Basics and Beyond*. 2nd ed. New York: Guilford, 2011.

Beck, Judith S. *Cognitive Therapy for Challenging Problems: What to Do When the Basics Don't Work*. New York: Guilford, 2005.

Burns, David D. *The Feeling Good Handbook*. New York: Plume, 1999.

Zucker, Bonnie. *Anxiety-Free Kids: An Interactive Guide for Parents and Children*. Waco, TX: Prufrock, 2008.

**What we THINK creates what we FEEL**

Zucker, *Anxiety-Free Kids*.

**Check out how a different way of thinking about the exact same situation**

Zucker, *Anxiety-Free Kids*.

**It's All in Your Head**

Mendelberg, Tali, Chris Karpowitz, and Lee Shaker. "Gender Inequality in Deliberative Participation." *American Political Science Review* 106, no. 3 (2012): 533–47. https://doi.org/10.1037/e511862012-001.

Schmader, Toni, and Brenda Major. "The Impact of Ingroup vs Outgroup Performance on Personal Values."

*Journal of Experimental Social Psychology* 35, no. 1 (1999): 47–67. https://doi.org/10.1006/jesp.1998.1372.

### Are male and female brains different?

For an overview on brain differences, we'd suggest the *The Female Brain*, by Louann Brizendine, or *Unleash the Power of the Female Brain*, by Daniel G. Amen. Also extremely helpful is the growing body of literature by researchers such as Gert de Vries, Patrica Boyle, Richard Simerly, Kelly Cosgrove, and Larry Cahill. And finally, this comprehensive review of literature is extremely helpful: check out Glenda E. Gillies and Simon McArthur's article "Estrogen Actions in the Brain and the Basis for Differential Action in Men and Women: A Case for Sex-Specific Medicines."

Achiron, R., and A. Achiron. "Development of the Human Fetal Corpus Callosum: A High-Resolution, Cross-Sectional Sonographic Study." *Ultrasound in Obstetrics and Gynecology* 18, no. 4 (2001): 343–47. https://doi.org/10.1046/j.0960-7692.2001.00512.x.

Amen, Daniel G. *Unleash the Power of the Female Brain: Supercharging Yours for Better Health, Energy, Mood, Focus, and Sex.* New York: Random House Digital, 2013.

Ankney, C. Davison. "Sex Differences in Relative

Brain Size: The Mismeasure of Woman, Too?" *Intelligence* 16, no. 3 (1992): 329–36. https://doi.org/10.1016/0160-2896(92)90013-h.

Apicella, C., A. Dreber, B. Campbell, P. Gray, M. Hoffman, and A. Little. "Testosterone and Financial Risk Preferences." *Evolution and Human Behavior* 29, no. 6 (2008): 384–90. https://doi.org/10.1016/j.evolhumbehav.2008.07.001.

Brizendine, Louann. *The Female Brain*. New York: Random House Digital, 2007.

Coates, J. M., and J. Herbert. "Endogenous Steroids and Financial Risk Taking on a London Trading Floor." *Proceedings of the National Academy of Sciences* 105, no. 16 (2008): 6167–72. https://doi.org/10.1073/pnas.0704025105.

Corbier, P., A. Edwards, and J. Roffi. "The Neonatal Testosterone Surge: A Comparative Study." *Archives of Physiology and Biochemistry* 100, no. 2 (1992): 127–31.

Evans, Alan C. "The NIH MRI Study of Normal Brain Development." *NeuroImage* 30, no. 1 (2006): 184–202. https://doi.org/10.1016/j.neuroimage.2005.09.068.

Gillies, Glenda E., and Simon McArthur. "Estrogen Actions in the Brain and the Basis for Differential Action in Men and Women: A Case for Sex-Specific

Medicines." *Pharmacological Reviews* 62, no. 2 (2010): 155–98. https://doi.org/10.1124/pr.109.002071.

Gurian, Michael. *Boys and Girls Learn Differently! A Guide for Teachers and Parents.* San Francisco: Jossey-Bass, 2011.

Haier, Richard J., Rex E. Jung, Ronald A. Yeo, Kevin Head, and Michael T. Alkire. "The Neuroanatomy of General Intelligence: Sex Matters." *NeuroImage* 25, no. 1 (2005): 320–27. https://doi.org/10.1016/j.neuroimage.2004.11.019.

Hsu, Jung-Lung. "Gender Differences and Age-Related White Matter Changes of the Human Brain: A Diffusion Tensor Imaging Study." *NeuroImage* 39, no. 2 (January 15, 2008): 566–77. https://doi.org/10.1016/j.neuroimage.2007.09.017.

Kanaan, Richard A., Matthew Allin, Marco Picchioni, Gareth J. Barker, Eileen Daly, Sukhwinder S. Shergill, James Woolley, and Philip K. Mcguire. "Gender Differences in White Matter Microstructure." *PLoS ONE* 7, no. 6 (2012). https://doi.org/10.1371/journal.pone.0038272.

Kilpatrick, L. A., D. H. Zald, J. V. Pardo, and L. F. Cahill. "Sex-Related Differences in Amygdala Functional Connectivity during Resting Conditions." *NeuroImage*

30, no. 2 (April 1, 2006): 452–61. https://doi.org/10.1016
/j.neuroimage.2005.09.065.

Kimura, Doreen. "Sex Differences in the Brain." *Scientific
American* 267, no. 3 (1992): 118–25.

Lemay, Marjorie, and Antonio Culebras. "Human
Brain—Morphologic Differences in the Hemispheres
Demonstrable by Carotid Arteriography." *New
England Journal of Medicine* 287, no. 4 (1972): 168–70.
https://doi.org/10.1056/nejm197207272870404.

Magon, Angela Josette. "Gender, the Brain and
Education: Do Boys and Girls Learn Differently?"
master's thesis, University of Victoria, 2009. http://
citeseerx.ist.psu.edu/viewdoc/download?doi=
10.1.1.456.6637&rep=rep1&type=pdf.

Reed, W. L., M. E. Clark, P. G. Parker, S. A. Raouf, N.
Arguedas, D. S. Monk, E. Snajdr, et al. "Physiological
Effects on Demography: A Long-Term Experimental
Study of Testosterone's Effects on Fitness." *American
Naturalist* 167, no. 5 (2006): 667–83. https://doi.
org/10.1086/503054.

Sacher, Julia, Jane Neumann, Hadas Okon-Singer, Sarah
Gotowiec, and Arno Villringer. "Sexual Dimorphism
in the Human Brain: Evidence from Neuroimaging."
*Magnetic Resonance Imaging* 31, no. 3 (April 2013):

366–75. https://doi.org/10.1016/j.mri.2012.06.007.

Takeuchi, Hikaru, Yasuyuki Taki, Yuko Sassa, Hiroshi Hashizume, Atsushi Sekiguchi, Tomomi Nagase, Rui Nouchi, et al. "White Matter Structures Associated with Emotional Intelligence: Evidence from Diffusion Tensor Imaging." *Human Brain Mapping* 34, no. 5 (2011): 1025–34. https://doi.org/10.1002/hbm.21492.

Wager, Tor D., K. Luan Phan, Israel Liberzon, and Stephan F. Taylor. "Valence, Gender, and Lateralization of Functional Brain Anatomy in Emotion: A Meta-analysis of Findings from Neuroimaging." *NeuroImage* 19, no. 3 (2003): 513–31. https://doi.org/10.1016/s1053-8119(03)00078-8.

## A fear of spiders (arachnophobia) is very common

Paul, Marla. "Touching Tarantulas." *Northwestern Now*, May 21, 2012. https://news.northwestern.edu/stories/2012/05/spider-phobia.

## Tell yourself the "maybe" story

Beck, *Cognitive Behavior Therapy*.

Clark, David A., and Aaron T. Beck. *The Anxiety and Worry Workbook: The Cognitive Behavioral Solution*. New York: Guilford, 2011.

### List past accomplishments

Amabile, Teresa M., and Richard J. Kramer. "The Power of Small Wins." *Harvard Business Review*, May 2011. http://yorkworks.ca/default/assets/File/PowerOfSmallWins(1).pdf.

### Look at positive images and think positive thoughts

Nittono, Hiroshi, Michiko Fukushima, Akihiro Yano, and Hiroki Moriya. "The Power of Kawaii: Viewing Cute Images Promotes a Careful Behavior and Narrows Attentional Focus." *PLoS One* 7, no. 9 (September 26, 2012). https://doi.org/10.1371/journal.pone.0046362.

### Hit the Pause button

Fredrickson, B. L., M. A. Cohn, K. A. Coffey, J. Pek, and S. M. Finkel. "Open Hearts Build Lives: Positive Emotions, Induced through Loving-Kindness Meditation, Build Consequential Personal Resources." *Journal of Personality and Social Psychology* 95, no. 5 (2008): 1045–62. https://doi.org/10.1037/a0013262.

Tang, Y.-Y., B. K. Hölzel, and M. I. Posner. "The Neuroscience of Mindfulness Meditation." *Nature Reviews Neuroscience* 16, no. 4 (2015): 213–25. https://doi.org/10.1038/nrn3916.

### Change the channel

"Understanding the Stress Response." Harvard Health.
Last updated March 18, 2016. www.health.harvard.
edu/staying-healthy/understanding-the-stress-response.

### Write down negative thoughts and then rip them up or throw them away

Briñol, Pablo, Margarita Gascó, Richard E. Petty, and
Javier Horcajo. "Treating Thoughts as Material
Objects Can Increase or Decrease Their Impact on
Evaluation." *Psychological Science* 24, no. 1 (2012):
41–7. https://doi.org/10.1177/0956797612449176.

### Gratitude Attitude

Watkins, P., K. Woodward, T. Stone, and R. Kolts.
"Gratitude and Happiness: Development of a Measure of
Gratitude and Relationships with Subjective Well-Being."
*Social Behavior and Personality: An International Journal*
31, no. 5 (August 2003): 431–52. https://doi.org/10.2224/
sbp.2003.31.5.431.

### Ride in a hot air balloon

Kearney, Christopher A. *Helping School Refusing
Children and Their Parents: A Guide for School-Based*

*Professionals.* Oxford: Oxford University Press, 2008.

## Chapter 6: Confident Friendship

### Scientists have discovered that friendship makes you stronger, healthier, and happier

Holt-Lunstad, Julianne, Timothy B. Smith, Mark Baker, Tyler Harris, and David Stephenson. "Loneliness and Social Isolation as Risk Factors for Mortality." *Perspectives on Psychological Science* 10, no. 2 (March 11, 2015): 227–37. https://doi.org/10.1177/1745691614568352.

Holt-Lunstad, Julianne, Timothy B. Smith, and J. Layton. "Social Relationships and Mortality Risk: A Meta-analytic Review." *PLOS Medicine* 7, no. 7 (July 2010).

### Friendship lowers your chance of heart disease

Gouin, Jean-Philippe, Biru Zhou, and Stephanie Fitzpatrick. "Social Integration Prospectively Predicts Changes in Heart Rate Variability Among Individuals Undergoing Migration Stress." *Annals of Behavioral Medicine* 49, no. 2 (2014): 230–38. https://doi.org/10.1007/s12160-014-9650-7.

### When you're around your friends, you pump out oxytocin

Taylor, S. E., L. C. Klein, B. P. Lewis, T. L. Gruenwald,

R. A. R. Gurung, and J. A. Updegraff. "Biobehavioral
Responses to Stress in Females: Tend-and-Befriend,
Not Fight-or-Flight." *Psychological Review* 107,
no. 3 (2002): 411–29. https://taylorlab.psych.ucla.
edu/wp-content/uploads/sites/5/2014/10/2000_
Biobehavioral-responses-to-stress-in-females_tend-
and-befriend.pdf.

**Not having strong friendships is as unhealthy as smoking**
Harvard Women's Health Watch. "The Health Benefits
of Strong Relationships." Harvard Health, December
2010. www.health.harvard.edu/newsletter_article/
the-health-benefits-of-strong-relationships.

**She'll be less stressed if she's got a friend there** and **Girls
who have even one good friend**
Adams, R. E., J. B. Santo, and W. M. Bukowski. "The
Presence of a Best Friend Buffers the Effects of
Negative Experiences." *Developmental Psychology*
47, no. 6 (2011): 1786–91. https://doi.org/10.1037/
a0025401.

**Research shows that a friend's behavior is contagious**
Christakis, N. A., and J. H. Fowler, "Social Contagion
Theory: Examining Dynamic Social Networks and

Human Behavior." *Statistics in Medicine* 32, no. 4
(February 20, 2013): 556–77. http://fowler.ucsd.edu/
social_contagion_theory.pdf.

**Girls' brains are wired to value their friends' approval**
Albert, Dustin, Jason Chein, and Laurence Steinberg.
"The Teenage Brain: Peer Influences on Adolescent
Decision Making." *Current Directions in Psychological
Science* 22, no. 2 (April 16, 2013): 114–20. https://doi.
org/10.1177/0963721412471347.

**Chapter 7: A Confident Girl's Guide to Navigating Screens**
**92 percent of teens are online every day**
Lenhart, Amanda. "Teens, Technology and Friendships."
Pew Research Center: Internet, Science & Tech.
August 6, 2015. www.pewinternet.org/2015/08/06/
teens-technology-and-friendships.

**50 percent of teens say they feel addicted to their phones**
Wallace, Kelly. "50% of Teens Feel Addicted to Their
Phones, Poll Says." CNN. July 29, 2016. www.cnn.
com/2016/05/03/health/teens-cell-phone-addiction-
parents/index.html.

**88 percent of teens think oversharing is a big issue** and **77%**
**of teens think they are less authentic**

Lenhart, "Teens, Technology and Friendships."

**One-third of all private pictures sent**

Lenhart, Amanda. "Chapter 5: Conflict, Friendships
and Technology." Pew Research Center: Internet,
Science & Tech. August 6, 2015. www.pewinternet.org
/2015/08/06chapter-5-conflict-friendships-and-
technology.

**Fun Fact: The Chocolate Alibi**

Sherman, Lauren E., Ashley A. Payton, Leanna M.
Hernandez, Patricia M. Greenfield, and Mirella
Dapretto. "The Power of the Like in Adolescence."
*Psychological Science* 27, no. 7 (2016): 1027–35. https://
doi.org/10.1177/0956797616645673.
Soat, Molly. "Social Media Triggers a Dopamine High."
*Marketing News*, November 2015. www.ama.org/
publications/MarketingNews/Pages/feeding-the-
addiction.aspx.

**Cyberbullying**

"Cyber Bullying Statistics." NoBullying—Bullying &

CyberBullying Resources. June 12, 2017. https://
nobullying.com/cyber-bullying-statistics-2014.

**Section 3: The Confident Self**

**Chapter 8: Kicking the Perfectionism Habit**

We learned a lot about perfectionism from these sources:

Homayoun, Ana. *The Myth of the Perfect Girl: Helping
Our Daughters Find Authentic Success and Happiness
in School and Life.* New York: Perigee, 2013.

Simmons, Rachel. *The Curse of the Good Girl: Raising
Authentic Girls with Courage and Confidence.* New
York: Penguin, 2010.

**If perfection is your goal**

Hewitt, Paul L., and Gordon L. Flett. "Perfectionism
in the Self and Social Contexts: Conceptualization,
Assessment, and Association with Psychopathology."
*Journal of Personality and Social Psychology* 60, no. 3
(1991): 456–70. https://doi.org/10.1037//0022-
3514.60.3.456.

**Girls and Perfectionism: A Super-Short Flowchart**

Dweck, *Mindset.*

**Perfectionism isn't the key to success.**

Hewitt, Paul L., and Gordon L. Flett. "Perfectionism in the Self and Social Contexts."

Lynd-Stevenson, "Perfectionism and depressive affect."

Marano, Hara Estroff. "Pitfalls of Perfectionism." *Psychology Today*, March 1, 2008. Updated June 9, 2016. www.psychologytoday.com/articles/200803/pitfalls-perfectionism.

Mitchelson, "Perfectionism."

Sullivan, Bob, and Hugh Thompson. *The Plateau Effect: Getting From Stuck to Success*. New York: Dutton, 2013.


**Perfectionism Cures**

Marano, "Pitfalls of Perfectionism."


**92 percent of teen girls would like to change something**

Antony, Martin M. "Cognitive-Behavioral Therapy for Perfectionism." Lecture, Anxiety and Depression Association of America, April 9, 2015. https://adaa.org/sites/default/files/Antony_MasterClinician.pdf.

"Statistics on Girls & Women's Self Esteem, Pressures & Leadership." Heart of Leadership. Accessed October 31, 2017. http://www.heartofleadership.org/statistics.

**Nine out of ten girls feel pressure by fashion and media industries to be skinny**

Girl Scouts of the USA/Girl Scout Research Institute. "Beauty Redefined: Girls and Body Image." 2010. www.girlscouts.org/content/dam/girlscouts-gsusa/ forms-and-documents/about-girl-scouts/research/ beauty_redefined_factsheet.pdf.

**53 percent of American girls unhappy with their bodies**

"Body Image and Nutrition." Teen Health and the Media. Accessed November 13, 2017. http://depts.washington .edu/thmedia/view.cgi?section=bodyimage&page= fastfacts.

**Eight in ten girls opt out of sports** and **Seven in ten girls don't want to assert themselves**

Dove Self-Esteem Project. "Girls and Beauty Confidence: The Global Report." 2017. www.unilever.com/Images/ dove-girls-beauty-confidence-report-infographic_ tcm244-511240_en.pdf.

**Chapter 9: Being True to You**
**Finding You**

Peterson, Christopher, and Martin E. P. Seligman.

*Character Strengths and Virtues: A Handbook and Classification.* Oxford: Oxford University Press, 2004.

Reckmeyer, Mary, and Jennifer Robison. *Strengths Based Parenting: Developing Your Children's Innate Talents.* New York: Gallup Press, 2016.

"The VIA Survey." Values in Action Institute. Accessed November 1, 2017. www.viacharacter.org/www/ Character-Strengths-Survey.

Waters, Lea. *The Strength Switch: How the New Science of Strength-Based Parenting Can Help Your Child and Your Teen to Flourish.* New York: Avery, 2017.

## Born That Way?

Duckworth, *Grit.*

Ericsson, K. Anders, Ralf T. Krampe, and Clemens Tesch-Romer. "The Role of Deliberate Practice in the Acquisition of Expert Performance." *Psychological Review* 100, no. 3 (1993): 363–406. https://graphics8. nytimes.com/images/blogs/freakonomics/pdf/ DeliberatePractice.

Gladwell, Malcolm. *Outliers: The Story of Success.* New York: Little, Brown, 2011.

**Chapter 10: Becoming a Girl of Action**

**The Science of Me to We**

Crocker, Jennifer, and Jessica Carnevale. "Self-Esteem
Can Be an Ego Trap." *Scientific American*, August
9, 2013. www.scientificamerican.com/article/
self-esteem-can-be-ego-trap.

Stulberg, Brad, and Steve Magness. "Be Better at Life by
Thinking of Yourself Less." *New York*, June 6, 2017.
http://nymag.com/scienceofus/2017/06/be-better-at-life-
by-thinking-of-yourself-less.html.

Stulberg, Brad, and Steve Magness. *Peak Performance:
Elevate Your Game, Avoid Burnout, and Thrive with
the New Science of Success.* Emmaus, PA: Rodale,
2017.


**Girls and women may be particularly drawn to the idea of
helping**

Soutschek, Alexander, Christopher J. Burke, Anjali Raja
Beharelle, Robert Schreiber, Susanna C. Weber,
Iliana I. Karipidis, Jolien Ten Velden, et al. "The
Dopaminergic Reward System Underpins Gender
Differences in Social Preferences." *Nature Human
Behaviour* 1, no. 11 (2017): 819–27. https://doi.
org/10.1038/s41562-017-0226-y.

**Prefer to work for a company that does something good for society**

"What Men, Women Value in a Job." Chap. 3 in "On Pay
Gap, Millennial Women Near Parity—For Now."
Pew Research Center's Social & Demographic Trends
Project. December 10, 2013. www.pewsocialtrends.
org/2013/12/11/chapter-3-what-men-women-value-
in-a-job.

**Goal Time**

Locke, Edwin A. "Motivation through Conscious
Goal Setting." *Applied and Preventive Psychology*
5, no. 2 (1996): 117–24. https://doi.org/10.1016/
s0962-1849(96)80005-9.

**Confidence is contagious**

Campbell-Meiklejohn, Daniel, Arndis Simonsen, Chris
D. Frith, and Nathaniel D. Daw. "Independent
Neural Computation of Value from Other People's
Confidence." *Journal of Neuroscience* 37, no. 3
(January 18, 2017): 673–84. https://doi.org/10.1523/
jneurosci.4490-15.2017.

"Science Proves Confidence Is Contagious." *Barron's*.
January 24, 2017. www.barrons.com/articles/

science-proves-confidence-is-contagious-1485216033.

Zomorodi, Manoush. "What Google Is Doing to Solve Its Gender Problem." *Note to Self* (podcast), April 29, 2015. www.wnyc.org/story/google-test-case-gender-bias.

**Women and girls are more willing to DO risky things**

Boschma, Janie. "Why Women Don't Run for Office." Politico. June 12, 2017. www.politico.com/ interactives/2017/women-rule-politics-graphic.

Our book was heavily supported by interviews with:

Lyn Brown, author of *Powered by Girl*, and director of Women's, Gender, and Sexuality Studies at Colby College

Phyllis Fagell, *Washington Post* columnist, psychologist, middle school parenting expert, and middle school counselor

Wanda Holland Greene, head of the Hamlin School for Girls

Craig Kielburger, cofounder of the WE organization

Rachel Simmons, author of *Odd Girl Out* and *Enough As She Is* and leadership development specialist at Smith College

Bonnie Zucker, psychologist and author of *Anxiety-Free Kids*

Our book was also heavily informed and inspired by the many lengthy interviews we conducted with dozens of scientists and experts about confidence for *The Confidence Code: The Science and Art of Self-Assurance—What Women Should Know* in 2014. Among them:

Cameron Anderson, University of California at Berkeley

Victoria Brescoll, Yale School of Management

Kenneth DeMarree, University of Buffalo

David Dunning, Cornell University

Joyce Ehrlinger, University of Washington

Rebecca Elliott, University of Manchester

Zach Estes, Bocconi University (Milan)

Christy Glass, Utah State University

Adam Kepecs, Cold Spring Harbor Labs

Dr. Jay Lombard, Genomind

Kristin Neff, University of Texas

Nansook Park, University of Michigan

Laura-Ann Petitto, Gallaudet University

Richard Petty, Ohio State University

Stephen Suomi, National Institute of Health

Barbara Tannenbaum, Brown University

Shelley Taylor, University of California at Los Angeles

**KATTY KAY** is the anchor of *BBC World News America*, based in Washington, DC. She is also a frequent contributor to *Meet the Press* and *Morning Joe* and a regular guest host of *The Diane Rehm Show* on NPR. In addition to her work on women's issues, Katty has covered the Clinton administration; four presidential elections; and the wars in Kosovo, Afghanistan, and Iraq. She was at the Pentagon just twenty minutes after a hijacked plane flew into the building on 9/11—one of her most vivid journalistic memories is of interviewing soldiers still visibly shaking from the attack. Katty grew up all over the Middle East, where her father was posted as a British diplomat. She studied modern languages at Oxford and is a fluent French and Italian speaker with some "rusty Japanese." Katty juggles her journalism with raising four children with her husband, a consultant.

**CLAIRE SHIPMAN** is a journalist, author, and public speaker. Before turning to writing, Claire spent fourteen years as a regular contributor to *Good Morning America* and other national broadcasts for ABC News. Prior to that, she served as White House correspondent for NBC News. She also worked for CNN for a decade, covering the White House, and was posted in Moscow for five years. She'll never forget the fall of the Soviet Union and watching ordinary citizens swarm city squares to pull down, with rope and a lot of anger, gigantic statues of the unpopular communist leaders. Her coverage helped CNN earn a Peabody Award. She also received a DuPont Award and an Emmy Award for coverage of the 1989 Tiananmen Square student uprising. She studied Russian at Columbia University and also earned a master's degree from the School of International Affairs there. She's now a member of Columbia's board of trustees. She lives in Washington, DC, with her husband, son, daughter, and a pack of dogs.

 **JILLELLYN RILEY** is a writer and editor with extensive experience in crafting and telling stories. She's worked with bestselling, innovative children's authors, as well as on nonfiction and fiction for adults. Her cowritten middle grade series is *The Saturday Cooking Club*. JillEllyn lives in Brooklyn, New York, with her husband, two sons, and canine ally Stella.

 **NAN LAWSON** is an illustrator and artist based in Los Angeles. She's a regular contributor to several art galleries across the country and has had the opportunity to work with companies such as the Academy Awards, Lucasfilm, Nickelodeon, and Hulu. She also works with freelance clients for animation visual development as well as book and editorial illustration. She spends most of her days drawing, drinking coffee, and romping around LA with her husband and daughter.